Zhitong Shangwu Yingyu Tuozhan Jiaocheng

Career Express Business English

职通商务英语

Extended Book

拓展教程 *3*

◎ 总主编　贺雪娟
◎ 主　编　许灵芝　文　平

高等教育出版社·北京
HIGHER EDUCATION PRESS BEIJING

图书在版编目（CIP）数据

职通商务英语拓展教程.3 / 贺雪娟主编；许灵芝，文平分册主编.
— 北京：高等教育出版社，2011.7
ISBN 978-7-04-032027-5

Ⅰ.①职… Ⅱ.①贺… ②许… ③文… Ⅲ.①商务−英语−高等
职业教育−教材 Ⅳ.① H31

中国版本图书馆 CIP 数据核字（2011）第 109242 号

策划编辑	闵 阅	责任编辑	康冬婷	封面设计 于 涛		版式设计 刘 艳
责任校对	康冬婷	责任印制	韩 刚			

出版发行	高等教育出版社	咨询电话	400−810−0598	
社　　址	北京市西城区德外大街4号	网　　址	http://www.hep.edu.cn	
邮政编码	100120		http://www.hep.com.cn	
印　　刷	北京鑫丰华彩印有限公司	网上订购	http://www.landraco.com	
开　　本	850×1168 1/16		http://www.landraco.com.cn	
印　　张	7.5	版　　次	2011年7月第1版	
字　　数	191 000	印　　次	2011年7月第1次印刷	
购书热线	010−58581118	定　　价	22.00元	

本书如有缺页、倒页、脱页等质量问题，请到所购图书销售部门联系调换

前　言

　　随着经济全球化的进一步发展，我国与世界各国的经济合作日益深入，国际商贸交往日益频繁。在对国际化商贸人才的需求日益增加的同时，社会对高素质商贸人才的英语应用能力的要求愈来愈高，进而对商务英语教学的载体——商务英语教材的编写也提出了更高的要求。《职通商务英语》系列教材旨在提高学习者的商务英语语言交际技巧，培养其熟练掌握英语、通晓商务知识、熟悉国际商务环境、善于跨文化交际的能力，以满足现代社会对商贸人才的需求。

商贸职业岗位群人才培养目标分析表

职业岗位群	主要工作岗位	人才培养目标
国际商务从业人员	进出口贸易，国际物流，国际金融，服务外包等岗位	培养熟练运用商务英语专业技能从事国际商务工作的应用型人才
涉外企业管理人员	涉外企业生产、销售、管理等岗位	培养以英语语言为工具在涉外企业从事生产、销售、管理工作的一线人才
涉外服务从业人员	外事接待、涉外旅游等岗位	培养能熟练运用英语从事外事接待、涉外旅游服务等服务三产一线的专门人才

　　《职通商务英语》系列教材将商务专业知识和跨文化商务交际能力与英语语言运用技能结合在一起，以学习者为中心、以商务为环境、以商贸岗位任务为路径、以商务交际为目的，由浅入深，循序渐进，通过对学习者听、说、读、写、译等基本技能的全面训练，使学习者掌握一定的商务技能，通晓英语知识培养他们在未来岗位中进行商务交际和完成商务任务的能力。

课程总目标	培养学习者在商务场景中使用英语语言知识和商务知识的技能，使学习者能够完成具体商务任务，成为适应社会需要的应用型涉外商务工作者。
商务知识与技能	使学习者了解和领悟商务活动中需要的知识，掌握商务活动中需要的技能，并灵活运用于商务实践。
语言知识与技能	使学习者通晓商务英语语言知识与技能，完成商务交际任务。

一.《职通商务英语》系列教材的特点

1. 分析岗位，设计系统

　　《职通商务英语》系列教材是在分析商贸职业人才培养目标，解构职业岗位的基础上，针对行业、企业对商贸高素质人才的要求完成单元主题及框架结构设计的。设计系统，适合高职高专经贸、商务专业的学习者使用。

2.选材真实，突出实用

本系列教材选材真实，编写组成员耗时一个多月，远赴国外著名大学及外贸机构进行选材。所有素材均采用真实事件、真实人物、真实案例，内容涉及企业管理、国际贸易、金融证券、商务礼仪等。通过大量真实、生动的素材，营造出真实的商务活动情境，满足学习者对商务英语学习的实际需求。

3.设计新颖，注重操作

本教程根据商务英语课程和高职高专学生特点，在教材设计中充分考虑教学法，运用行动导向教育理念和ISAS（Information Search and Analysis Skills）等新的教学观念和手段，注重语言的交际功能和商务知识的应用，遵循"输入—内化—输出"的学习规律，强调教与学的紧密结合。

4.三位一体，凸显完美

本系列教材由综合教程、听说教程和拓展教程三部分组成。综合教程和教师参考书提供了各单元的主题课文、课文练习、课堂教学设计、课文分析、语法讲解、写作技巧、练习答案以及大量商务背景资料；听力教程和教师参考书提供了大量取材于真实商务活动的英语听说训练和商务背景知识介绍，旨在进一步强化听说能力的学习和提高；拓展教程由词汇、语法、阅读、写作及商务技能几部分组成，供学生课后进行巩固及拓展性练习。本系列教材配有电子教案、MP3录音、网络资源等相关教学资源，提供了教学各环节所需要的素材，并定期更新。

5.循序渐进，强化阶段

本系列教材共分为4册，内容从基本商务概念、理论到具体商务操作流程以及实际案例分析，便于学习者循序渐进地完成各阶段商务英语知识的学习，更具目的性和科学性。

二.《职通商务英语》系列教材的结构：

《职通商务英语》系列教材共分4册，第一册、第二册旨在培养学生的词汇、语法、语用技能、跨文化交际能力和普通商务知识；第三册围绕国际商务及国际贸易流程设计单元主题，进一步培养学生的语言实际运用能力及专业商务知识；第四册为具体商务案例的学习与分析。

《职通商务英语》系列教材构成图

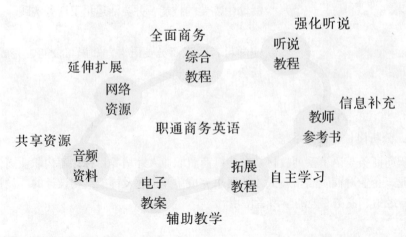

　　《职通商务英语综合教程》配备MP3录音，每册包含10个教学单元和3个复习单元，各教学单元体例统一，都由以下5个模块构成：

　　　　学习目标（语言技能、语法要点、词汇、商务交际）；

　　　　任务导入（小组讨论、问题回答、意见陈述、热身练习）；

　　　　精读课文（导语、阅读前任务、课文、注释、阅读理解）；

　　　　语言要点（词汇与语法、商务技巧、商务翻译）；

　　　　商务交际（商务写作、商务听说、商务礼仪）。

　　《职通商务英语教师参考书》摆脱了传统的教参编排方式，力求从教师角度出发，做到信息丰富，设计合理，使用方便。电子教案是课堂教学的重要辅助资料，每册分为10个单元，每单元分为一个主页面和三个教学板块，结构清晰，便于教师操作。图文并茂的形式，也有利于激发学生的学习热情。

　　《职通商务英语听说教程》配备MP3录音，每册包含10个教学单元，各单元的主题与《综合教程》有所不同但相互关联，旨在强化学习者的商务英语听说能力。

　　《职通商务英语拓展教程》是《综合教程》的补充和扩展，力求从方便学生自学的角度出发，提供与单元主题相关的自测习题，可作为课后练习来检测学生的学习效果，部分内容还可用于丰富课堂教学。

　　《职通商务英语》系列教材由长沙民政职业技术学院应用外语系主任贺雪娟教授担任总主编。《职通商务英语拓展教程3》的主编为长沙民政职业技术学院的许灵芝、文平，参与编写此书的其他编者包括邓曼英、刘玉丹、金钏、李琰、陈懿、李涵、杨亮辉、李兰、朱毅恒。大连理工大学的孔庆炎教授担任了《职通商务英语》系列教材的总主审。

　　本套教材在内容设计和材料选取上均作了不少新的尝试，编者真诚地希望使用本教材的学生和教师能对教材的不足之处提出宝贵意见，以便我们今后加以完善。

编　者

2011年5月

拓展教程使用说明

一、编写说明

  《职通商务英语拓展教程3》是《职通商务英语综合教程3》的完美补充。提供了与主教材各单元主题相关的自测习题，可作为学生的课后练习及测试题，部分内容还可用于课堂教学。《职通商务英语拓展教程3》紧扣单元主题，是学生课堂学习过程的延续；同时又对相关语言知识进行了引申，对商务专业知识进行了拓展，旨在巩固、提高学生的语言技能，拓展学生的商务知识，训练学生的商务技巧。此外，为了帮助学生参加相关的英语考试，还增加了大学英语四级考试、剑桥商务英语考试和全国商务英语等级考试的题型，以激发学生的学习热情。

二、使用说明

  《职通商务英语拓展教程3》每单元分为语言应用能力、阅读理解能力、商务实践能力三个部分。

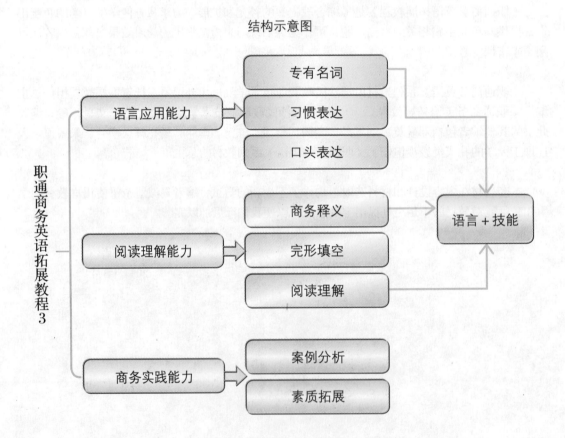

结构示意图

一、语言应用能力

1. 专有名词

   该部分提供了针对各单元重要词汇和商务术语的训练，通过英文释义和中英对照的搭配练习，帮助学生巩固词汇量，掌握商务术语。

2. 习惯表达

   该部分提供了针对各单元重点单词、短语、术语、专有名词、习惯用法、商务固有表达的习题，旨在帮助学生进一步学习和了解重难点词汇在商务领域中的运用。

3. 口头表达

   该部分提供了两个与单元主题相关的口头表达习题，形式多样，既有补充对话，也有口头任务，目的是使学习者在掌握一定词汇的基础上完成简单的商务交际任务。

二、阅读理解能力

1. 商务释义

   该部分借鉴了剑桥商务英语考试的题型，即要求学习者根据各单元所学知识，判断各段文字所描述的专业名词或商务现象。旨在帮助学习者在理解的基础上融会贯通地使用所学商务知识。

2. 完形填空

   该部分提供了一篇与单元主题相关，并在课文学习中已有阐述的文字。要求学习者结合课堂所学，同时利用词汇、语法、习惯用法等知识补全短文。目的是帮助学习者有效消化课堂所学，并与日常积累知识结合起来完成阅读任务。

3. 阅读理解

   该部分供学习者阅读理解及扩充相关商务知识。每单元提供两篇与单元主题相关的短文，帮助学生了解商务知识、掌握商务技能。

三、商务实践能力

1. 案例分析

   该部分提供一个与单元主题相关的案例，案例所涉及的知识或技能已经在课文学习中传授。目的是测试学习者能否根据所学商务知识解决真实商务问题，同时也为下一阶段学习搭建一个桥梁。

2. 素质拓展

   该部分提供一个与单元主题相关的素质拓展练习，主要为写作练习。既有直接给出主要信息点的形式，也有图表的形式。目的是测试学习者的写作水平，同时也能体现学习者的综合素质。

Contents

Trade Practice

1 Match the following trade terms with the Chinese equivalents.

1. FOB Liner Terms
2. FOB Stowed
3. FOB Trimmed
4. FOB Under Tackle
5. CIF Liner Terms
6. CIF Landed
7. CIF EX Ship's Hold

A. 装运港船上吊钩交货
B. 含平舱费装运港船上交货
C. 班轮条件下成本保险加运费
D. 成本保险加运费卸货到岸
E. 成本保险加运费舱底交货
F. 含理舱费装运港船上交货
G. 班轮条件下装运港船上交货

2 Choose the best answers.

1. The term CIF should be followed by _____.
   A. the point of origin   B. the port of shipment
   C. the port of destination   D. the port of exportation

2. The term FOB should be followed by _____.
   A. the point of origin   B. the port of importation
   C. the port of discharge   D. the port of exportation

3. The term EXW should be followed by _____.
   A. the point of premise   B. the port of shipment
   C. the port of importation   D. the port of exportation

4. The term DEQ should be followed by _____.
   A. the point of origin   B. the port of loading
   C. the port of destination   D. the port of shipment

5. The term FAS should be followed by _____.
   A. the point of origin   B. the port of destination
   C. the port of shipment   D. the port of importation

6. The term CFR should be followed by _____.
    A. the point of origin   B. the port of shipment
    C. the port of destination   D. the port of importation

7. The term DDP should be followed by _____.
    A. the point of origin   B. the port of shipment
    C. the port of premise   D. the place of destination

8. The term DES should be followed by _____.
    A. the point of origin   B. the port of importation
    C. the port of exportation   D. the port of shipment

9. The term DAF should be followed by _____.
    A. the point of origin   B. the port of importation
    C. the port of shipment   D. the place of destination

10. The term FCA should be followed by _____.
    A. the seller's railway station   B. the point of origin
    C. the seller's place of shipment   D. the buyer's railway station

③ Complete the following dialogues and practice them with your partner.

——Dialogue ①

> A. obligations   B. shipment   C. trade terms   D. responsibilities   E. nature

A: I am often at loss as to the meaning of _____1_____, for example, FOB, CFR and CIF. What are they used for?

B: In international trade, we usually make use of certain trade terms to define the _____2_____ of the contract, such as FOB contract, CFR contract and CIF contract, to determine expenses and risks as well as the responsibilities and _____3_____ accordingly.

A: So all other clauses in the contract shall be in conformity with the trade terms. Is it right?

B: Certainly. FOB, CFR and CIF are most commonly used in international trade. Let's start with FOB, and then you will understand the other two easily. FOB means Free On Board a vessel. In FOB Shanghai, Shanghai is the named port of _____4_____. It means that the seller fulfills his obligation when the goods have passed over the ship's rail at the named port of shipment. Remember, the seller must notify the buyer in good time that the goods have been on board.

A: Then who will be responsible for the shipment and insurance?

B: Under FOB, the buyer must be responsible for chartering a ship or booking the shipping space. It is also the buyer's _____5_____ to take out insurance.

A: Oh, I see. I think I have a brief idea about trade terms now. Thanks.

Dialogue ②

> A. the introduction of articles covering definitions and interpretations
> B. banks and the meaning of specific terms and events
> C. UCP 600 has really changed a lot
> D. could lead to inconsistent application and interpretation
> E. to address developments in the banking, transport and insurance industries

A: Hi, what's the book you are looking for?

B: I am a little confused.

A: What's wrong?

B: I have read UCP 600 recently, but I don't understand some terms.

A: Well, compared with UCP 500, _____6_____. So you should know the differences between these two versions.

B: I see. I have found that one of the structural changes to the UCP is _____7_____.

A: Yes. UCP 600 avoids repeated expression in providing definitions of roles played by _____8_____.

B: Similarly, the interpretation aims to take the ambiguity out of vague or unclear language that appears in L/C and to provide a definitive explanation of other features.

A: You really catch what I say. We all know the general objective of UCP 600 is _____9_____. Additionally, there was a need to look at the language and style used in the UCP to remove wording that _____10_____.

B: I think I should find some reference books related to the revision of UCP to get a thorough understanding.

A: OK.

 Read the following passages and decide which trade term each passage is describing.

| 1. EXW ( ) | 2. FOB ( ) | 3. CIF ( ) | 4. CFR ( ) | 5. DDP ( ) |

A. This trade term means the seller fulfills his obligation to deliver when the goods have been made available at the named place in the country of importation. The seller has to bear all the costs and risks involved in bringing the goods thereto including, where applicable, any duty for import in the country of destination.

B. This trade term means the seller delivers when he places the goods at the disposal of the buyer at the seller's premises or another named place not cleared for export and not loaded on any collecting vehicle.

C. This term is a popular cargo delivery arrangement and can only be used for sea and inland waterway transportation. And it requires the seller to clear the goods for export. The risk and any additional costs due to events happening after the time of delivery are transferred from the seller to the buyer.

D. This trade term pertains to the shipping of goods. It specifies which party pays for shipment and loading costs, and / or where responsibility for the goods is transferred. Buyer is responsible for all the costs incurred after the cargo has been loaded on board.

E. A trade term requiring the seller to arrange for the carriage of goods by sea to a port of destination, and provide the buyer with the documents necessary to obtain the goods from the carrier. Generally speaking, importers prefer this term when either they're new to international trade or they have relatively little freight volume. These importers often find it simpler in that their suppliers are responsible for arranging freight and insurance details.

 Read the passage and fill in the blanks.

The growth ____1____ international trade made it necessary to establish a ____2____ set of rules to provide the parties with certainty and security in their transactions. The UCP has been ____3____ approximately every 10 years in order to keep its ____4____ with current trade and banking customs and practices.

The 6th revision of the UCP was approved by the ICC Banking Commission on October 25, 2006 and was ____5____ force from July 1, 2007. This last ____6____ was led by a Drafting Group of nine members, eight of which were bankers and ____7____ a legal advisor for a bank with a large practice on documentary credits. The ____8____ process followed a traditional ____9____ through which the Drafting Group received ____10____ from the 120 national committees and when the comments showed a need of change on the rules the Drafting Group provided with a proposal or draft of such required changes.

In ____11____, we look at the drafting of UCP 500 which followed a slightly different methodology, one which differed from all of the previous revisions of the UCP. There

1. A. at   B. of
   C. in   D. from
2. A. full   B. whole
   C. generalized   D. gentle
3. A. downloaded   B. examined
   C. updated   D. renewed
4. A. priority   B. difference
   C. prestige   D. consistency
5. A. in   B. at
   C. on   D. to
6. A. chapter   B. revision
   C. article   D. group
7. A. of   B. for
   C. in   D. with
8. A. drafting   B. negotiating
   C. consulting   D. studying
9. A. content   B. direction
   C. methodology   D. policy
10. A. compliments B. criticism
    C. comments   D. gossip
11. A. order   B. contrast
    C. the way   D. sight

was a full revision of the articles of UCP 400 divided into two main groups, one which ___12___ with the "legal articles" and the other one with the documentary requirements. Its drafting also involved the work of lawyers and ___13___ in order to assure ___14___ of the two different perspectives of documentary credits.

　　Keeping the UCP as a living law is not the easiest job and one can be misled by ___15___ banking practices that can hinder the stability and ___16___ of documentary credits. Thus, either way of drafting the UCP rules can produce ___17___ results that are compatible with the current needs of the ___18___ involved in documentary credits, as long as they are focused in ___19___ the principles set by the UCP and the ISBP. This will only be ___20___ once the UCP is in force and in use, for now the only possibility is to review the changes and see its compliance with the standards and principles.

12. A. coped　　　　B. worked
　　C. corporate　　D. dealt
13. A. Prime Ministers　B. bankers
　　C. traders　　　D. politicians
14. A. security　　　B. clarity
　　C. compliance　　D. coverage
15. A. advanced　　B. strict
　　C. pathological　D. lagging
16. A. trustworthiness
　　B. improvement
　　C. inefficiency
　　D. durability
17. A. poor　　　　B. terrible
　　C. excellent　　D. different
18. A. nations　　　B. parties
　　C. countries　　D. groups
19. A. getting rid of　B. giving up
　　C. facing with　　D. maintaining
20. A. imaginable　　B. foreseeable
　　C. measurable　　D. enable

6 Read the following passage and choose the best answers.

　　In economics, absolute advantage refers to the ability of a party to produce more of a good or service than competitors, using the same amount of resources. A party with an absolute advantage when using the same input as another party can produce a greater output. Since absolute advantage is determined by a simple comparison of labor productivities, it is possible for a party to have no absolute advantage in anything; in that case, according to the theory of absolute advantage, no trade will occur with the other party. Generally, in international trade, countries export goods and services for which they have an absolute advantage and import goods and services for which another country has the absolute advantage.

　　It can be contrasted with the concept of comparative advantage which refers to the ability to produce a particular good at a lower opportunity cost. It is the ability to produce a product with the highest relative efficiency given all the other products that could be produced.

　　Comparative advantage explains how trade can create value for both parties even when one can produce all goods with fewer resources than the other. The net benefits of such an outcome are called gains from trade. It is the main concept of the pure theory of international trade.

   Absolute advantage and comparative advantage are two basic concepts to international trade. Under absolute advantage, one country can produce more output per unit of productive input than another. With comparative advantage, if one country has an absolute advantage in every type of output, the other might benefit from specializing in and exporting those products, if any exist.

   A country has an absolute advantage economically over another, in a particular good, when it can produce that good at a lower cost. Using the same input of resources, a country with an absolute advantage will have greater output. Assuming one good is the only item in the market, beneficial trade is impossible. An absolute advantage is one where trade is not mutually beneficial, as opposed to a comparative advantage where trade is mutually beneficial.

   A country has a comparative advantage in the production of a good if it can produce that good at a lower opportunity cost relative to another country. What matters is not the absolute cost of production but the opportunity cost, which measures how much production of one good is reduced to produce one more unit of the other good.

1. A party may have no absolute advantage in anything because _____.
   A. every party uses the same amount of resources
   B. it is decided by the ratio of the quantity and quality of units produced
   C. it produces more of a good or service than its competitor
   D. it uses the same input
2. Which of the following statements is TRUE according to the passage?
   A. In international trade, countries export goods and services for which another country has the absolute advantage.
   B. Countries import goods and services for which they have an absolute advantage.
   C. Comparative advantage means the ability to produce a product with the higher efficiency than other competitors.
   D. Trade can be mutually beneficial for both parties even when one can produce all goods with highest efficiency.
3. With comparative advantage, if one country has an absolute advantage in every type of output, the other _____.
   A. will get no gain from the trade at all
   B. can produce more output
   C. might get profits in specializing in and exporting some products
   D. will use the same amount of input
4. A country has a comparative advantage _____.
   A. if it can produce a product with the highest efficiency
   B. when it can produce all goods with fewer resources than the others
   C. on condition it can gain profits from trade
   D. if it can produce that good at a relatively lower opportunity cost than others

5. The opportunity cost refers to _____.
   A. the way to estimate the reduction of production in manufacturing goods
   B. the mutually beneficial trade
   C. a simple comparison of labor productivity
   D. the ability to produce a particular good at a lower cost

 Read the following passage and answer the questions.

National committees and groups form the global network that makes ICC unique among business organizations. ICC members shape the organization's policies and, through their national committees, alert their governments to international business concerns. In countries where a national committee has yet to be formed, companies can join ICC individually by becoming a direct member.

Incoterms rules explain standard terms that are used in contracts for the sale of goods. They are essential ICC tools that help traders avoid misunderstandings by clarifying the costs, risks, and responsibilities of both buyers and sellers.

Because the rules are developed by experts and practitioners brought together by ICC, and involve a long consultative process, they are globally accepted and have become the standard in international business rules setting.

On 27 – 29 September, for a one-off launch conference and the first of ICC headquarters' series of practical master classes on the Incoterms 2010 rules, members of the Incoterms Drafting Group will give a detailed public presentation of the new rules and demonstrate through case-studies the major changes and processes that users will need to know in their everyday practice.

The revision, the first in a decade, reflects the profound changes that have taken place in global trade since 2000. These include the increased importance of cargo security, the resulting new obligations on traders, developments in container transport, and the 2004 revision of the United States' Uniform Commercial Code, which resulted in a deletion of the former U.S. shipment and delivery terms.

The launch conference and master classes will address these and other changes, and will offer drafting tips, real life examples of the rules in action, and feedback from the key experts involved in elaborating the rules.

"These launch events are a unique opportunity for trade professionals to learn the fundamentals of the new Incoterms 2010 rules from the drafters themselves," said Emily O'Connor, ICC Senior Policy Manager and Secretariat for the Drafting Group. "There is no organization better placed than ICC — the organization that created and maintains the Incoterms rules — to help traders learn how to apply the rules correctly to their global or domestic sales transactions."

The launch conference and master classes should be of particular interest to contract/execution managers involved in the export/import of goods, trade finance officers, in-house freight and carriage operatives, in-house insurance specialists, commercial lawyers, and anyone interested in learning about the changes to the Incoterms rules.

Incoterms 2010, will come into effect on 1 January 2011.

1. What makes ICC unique among business organizations?

   _____.

2. What's the function of ICC members?

   _____.

3. Why Incoterms are globally accepted and have become the standard in international business rules setting?

   _____.

4. What do Incoterms 2010 reflect?

   _____.

5. What is the purpose of the passage?

   _____.

8 Translate the following sentences into Chinese.

1. An authenticated teletransmission of a credit or amendment will be deemed to be the operative credit or amendment, and any subsequent mail confirmation shall be disregarded.

   _____

   _____

2. If a teletransmission states "full details to follow" (or words of similar effect), or states that the mail confirmation is to be the operative credit or amendment, then the teletransmission will not be deemed to be the operative credit or amendment.

   _____

   _____

3. A document may be dated prior to the issuance date of the credit, but must not be dated later than its date of presentation.

   _____

   _____

4. At least one original of each document stipulated in the credit must be presented.

   _____

   _____

5. The date of issuance of the bill of lading will be deemed to be the date of shipment unless the bill of lading contains an on board notation indicating the date of shipment, in which case the date stated in the on board notation will be deemed to be the date of shipment.

_____

_____

 Read and answer the questions raised for this case.

Case : CFR & Shipping Notice

Fact: Company A entered into a contract with a foreign company B on towel under CFR terms. On the morning of the contracted date, the goods were all loaded onto the named vessel. The export salesperson of A sent the buyer the shipping advice the next morning. B immediately went to the local insurance company to insure the goods, the latter had already learned that the ship suffered a wreck the night before and refused to underwrite. B then sent a telex to A saying that "owing to your delayed notice of shipment, we are unable to insure the goods. Since the vessel has been destroyed in a wreck, the loss of goods should be for your account. You should also compensate our profit and expenses as listed below." B also refused to take up the shipping documents.

Question: In your opinion, did B have the right to do so? Why?

 Extended Exercise

Find out the discrepancies according to UCP600 in the following L/C.

SEQUENCE OF TOTAL *27: 1/1

FORM OF DOC. CREDIT *40 A: REVOCABLE

DOC. CREDIT NUMBER *20: DC123456

DATE OF ISSUE 31C: 13/4/2010

EXPIRY 31D: 13/5/2010

APPLICANT 50: ABC. Ltd

BENEFICIARY 59: ShengLi Inc.

AMOUNT 32B: CURRENCY USD AMOUNT 100,000

AVAILABLE WITH/BY 41D: ANY PRIME BANK IN CHINA BY NEGOTIATION

DRAFTS AT ... 42C: SIGHT

PARTIAL SHIPMENTS 43PERMITTED

TRANSSHIPMENT 43T: NOT PERMITTED

LOADING IN CHARGE 44A: ANY CHINA PORT

FOR TRANSPORT TO 44B: New York USA

LATEST DATE OF SHIP 44C: 13/5/2010

① Match the words with their corresponding definitions.

1. sanction
2. complementary
3. endorse

4. quota
5. formidable
6. surplus

7. labor-intensive
8. rebate

A. extremely impressive in strength or excellence
B. a quantity much larger than is needed
C. requiring a large expenditure of labor but not much capital

D. give support or one's approval to
E. a refund of some fraction of the amount paid
F. acting as or providing a complement (something that completes the whole)

G. a proportional share assigned to each participant
H. formal and explicit approval

② Choose the best answers.

1. China adopted its reform and opening policy in _____.
   A. 1981   B. 1978
   C. 2001   D. 2002
2. China formally joined the WTO in _____.
   A. 1981   B. 1978
   C. 2001   D. 2002
3. China's trade performance was better than expected in _____ since joining the WTO.
   A. 1981   B. 1978
   C. 2001   D. 2002
4. The main motivation in reforming China's trade policy is _____.
   A. comparative advantage   B. domestic need
   C. industrial competitiveness   D. regionalism

5. Since China acceded to the WTO, what is still the basis of its official policy is _____.
   A. comparative advantage   B. protectionism
   C. industrial competitiveness   D. regionalism
6. The cost of labor is the only advantage that Chinese enterprises enjoy in _____.
   A. comparative advantage   B. domestic need
   C. industrial competitiveness   D. regionalism
7. In some cases, it will be possible to _____ the requirements by adapting existing management system elements.
   A. comply with   B. comply to
   C. apply to   D. apply for
8. Russia is trying its best to accede _____ the WTO.
   A. in   B. for
   C. with   D. to
9. For several reasons, China's position in _____ is considered to be of great benefit.
   A. regionalism   B. globalization
   C. protectionism   D. free trade
10. The IMF will often ask these nations to take steps to decrease their imports or perhaps _____ their currencies.
    A. increase   B. depreciate
    C. inflate   D. downplay

③ Complete the following dialogues and practice them with your partner.

Dialogue ①

A. manifestation   B. institution   C. protectionist   D. accumulation   E. necessarily

A: Politicians and scholars talk and write about "trade policy", but they rarely explain what they mean. Can you tell me what trade policy actually means?

B: Let me see. "Trade policy" refers to the _____1_____ of deliberate government choices to express positions and preferences in international trade.

A: Oh! Then are there any _____2_____ for "trade policy"?

B: Certainly. "Trade policy" has essentially three manifestations: in the laws and _____3_____ of a country pertaining to trade; in the actions a country takes, pursuant to its laws, to restrict trade with respect to specific products or services; and in the negotiations a country undertakes to liberalize trade. As in all domains, policy must be understood as to what a country does, not _____4_____ what it says. It is politically correct everywhere to champion free trade.

A: I'm clearer about "trade policy" now. It is in favor of free trade.

B: But broadly speaking, trade policy is thought to be either in favor of free exchange, or to be _____5_____, favoring imports or domestic manufacture. Favoring imports, in turn, favors consumers because imports increase competition, expand the variety of products offered, and lower prices. Favoring domestic manufacture, however, generally is thought to defend jobs, and jobs, in the end, are at the heart of every trade policy.

A: Oh, thank you very much!

B: You are welcome.

——Dialogue ②

> A. Here I'll tell you three components of trade policy
>
> B. in the negotiations pursued to reduce tariff and other trade barriers
>
> C. What's the objective of trade negotiations
>
> D. because they have the most specific impact on trade partners
>
> E. but they alone do not constitute trade policy

A: Professor, What is the relationship between trade laws and trade policy?

B: Trade laws define the rules, _____6_____.

A: Then what's the function of the rules?

B: The rules permit domestic agencies to investigate allegations of unfair trade, and to impose restrictions on goods or services found to be unfairly traded.

A: Well, What is the most important feature of trade policy? And why?

B: The investigations, and the restrictions imposed, are probably the most important features of trade policy, _____7_____. They determine the continuous tensions among countries over trade.

A: I know trade policy has three manifestations. How about the other one?

B: The third, remaining manifestation of trade policy is _____8_____, and in the choice between bilateral and multilateral negotiations.

A: _____9_____?

B: The objectives of trade negotiations are always broadly the same: to reduce tariffs and trade barriers and generally to liberalize trade. However, domestic forces driven by the need and desire to protect jobs seek to protect certain sectors and thereby to limit liberalization.

A: Oh. Yesterday, Professor Smith discussed three manifestations. Is there anything related with trade policy?

B: Of course. There are too many. _____10_____. They are institutions (including laws and regulations); trade remedies (investigations and imposed trade restrictions); and trade negotiations.

Read the following sentences and passages and decide which passage each sentence is describing?

1. The country's exports in agriculture remain very important in the late 20th century. (   )
2. This international organization gives financial assistance to those countries with financial difficulties. (   )
3. Increasing export contributes to a country's rapid growth in economy. (   )
4. A good trade policy can improve development and decrease poverty. (   )
5. What is described in the passage is called protectionism. (   )

A. Trade rules are multilateral, but trade itself is bilateral — between buyers and sellers, exporters and importers. This is why the European Union has developed a network of bilateral trade agreements with individual countries and regions across the world. The enlargement of the EU from 15 to 27 members gives it added weight as a trading partner, particularly with its neighbors in Eastern Europe and the Mediterranean basin. The EU's trade policy is closely linked to its development policy. The two come together as the Union assumes its share of responsibility to help developing countries fight poverty and integrate into the global economy.

B. The concept of a "safeguard" in international trade is based on enabling industries facing a surge in imports from foreign countries to adjust to new market circumstances. A safeguard remedy is temporary, designed more to assist a besieged industry than to punish a foreign one because there is no legal basis for punishment — a safeguard does not involve any examination as to whether a foreign product is fairly traded. It matters only that exports are surging and that the surge injures domestic industry. Safeguards are exceptional trade remedies for two reasons: they do not require unfair trading, and they may result in a quota or tariff rate quota. Quotas in all forms are otherwise banned by international trade rules. They are permissible only as a remedy in a safeguard action.

C. China is now one of the most important markets for U.S. exports: in 2009, U.S. exports to China totaled $69.6 billion, a 0.2% decrease from 2008. Those percentages were down far less than U.S. exports to other major trading partners in the year following the global financial crisis. U.S. agricultural exports continue to play a major role in bilateral trade, totaling $12.2 billion in 2009 and thus making China the United States' fourth-largest agricultural export market. Leading categories include: soybeans ($7.3 billion), cotton ($839 million), and hides and skins ($713 million).

D. Export growth continues to play an important role in China's rapid economic growth. To increase exports, China has pursued policies such as fostering the rapid development of foreign-invested factories, which assemble imported components into consumer goods for export, and liberalizing trading rights. Since the adoption of the 11th Five-Year Program in 2005, however, China has placed greater emphasis on developing a consumer demand-driven economy to sustain economic growth and address global imbalances.

E. To help countries with unmanageable balance-of-payments problems, the Bretton Woods conference created the International Monetary Fund (IMF). The IMF extends short-term credit to nations unable to meet their debts through conventional means (generally, by increasing exports, taking out long-term loans, or using reserves). The IMF, to which the United States contributed 25 percent of an initial $8 800 million in capital, often requires chronic debtor nations to undertake economic reforms as a condition for receiving its short-term assistance.

5 Read the passage and fill in the blanks.

We have seen that domestic politics often causes countries to try to ____1____ their domestic firms from foreign ____2____ by erecting barriers to trade. Such forms of government ____3____ can be divided into two categories: tariffs and nontariff barriers. Countries have been ____4____ trade barriers since the creation of the modern nation-state in the sixteenth century in hopes of increasing national income, promoting economic ____5____, and/or raising their citizens' standard of living. Sometimes national trade policies that benefit special interest groups ____6____ at the expense of the general public or society ____7____.

A tariff is a tax placed on a good that is traded ____8____. Some tariffs are levied on goods as they leave the country (an export tariff) or as they pass ____9____ one country bound for another (a transit tariff). Most, however, are collected on ____10____ goods (an import tariff). In practice, most tariffs imposed by developed countries are ad valorem. The tariff applies to the product's value, which is typically the sales price ____11____ the product enters the country. The tariff code is very complicated, and an importer's expected profit margin on a transaction can shrink or disappear if a customs ____12____ subjects the imported goods to a higher tariff rate than the importer expected.

1. A. protect   B. prevent
   C. forbid   D. stop
2. A. importers   B. competitors
   C. countries   D. firms
3. A. way   B. intervention
   C. prevention   D. method
4. A. made   B. making
   C. erected   D. erecting
5. A. rise   B. drop
   C. growth   D. grow
6. A. is adopted   B. was adopted
   C. are adopted   D. were adopted
7. A. at large   B. in large
   C. at level   D. in level
8. A. nationally   B. internationally
   C. purposefully   D. domestically
9. A. by   B. on
   C. through   D. at
10. A. imported   B. exported
    C. transmitted   D. produced
11. A. in which   B. on which
    C. at which   D. of which
12. A. officer   B. official
    C. worker   D. clerk

Nontariff barriers are the second ____13____ of governmental controls on international trade. Any government regulation, policy, or procedure other than a tariff that has the effect of impeding international trade may be ____14____ a nontariff barrier (NTB). There are three kinds of NTBs: ____15____, numerical export controls, and other nontariff barriers. Countries may ____16____ international trade by imposing quotas. A quota is a numerical ____17____ on the quantity of a good that may be imported into a country during some time period, such as a year. A country also may ____18____ quantitative barriers to trade in the form of numerical limits on the amount of a good it will export. A voluntary export ____19____ (VER) is a promise by a country to a limit its ____20____ of a good to another country to a prespecified amount or percentage of the affected market.

13. A. kind   B. one
    C. type   D. category
14. A. labeled   B. made
    C. given   D. taken
15. A. tariffs   B. quotas
    C. nontariffs   D. barriers
16. A. restrain   B. prohibit
    C. keep   D. hold
17. A. limitation   B. control
    C. limit   D. figure
18. A. set   B. make
    C. carry out   D. impose
19. A. restraint   B. rise
    C. raise   D. rate
20. A. imports   B. exports
    C. production   D. transmission

 Read the following passage and choose the best answers.

Developing countries historically fear free markets, especially in agriculture, because developed countries can overwhelm developing markets. The characterization of developing countries, however, has become more complicated and nuanced as countries develop at different rates and reach different stages of development. These differences lead to different views of trade.

"Developing" and "developed" here are economic terms. They refer to the construction, maintenance, and operation of infrastructure, to the production of increasingly sophisticated goods and services, and to the opening of markets. Over the last decade, certain major developing countries, particularly Brazil, China, and India, have separated themselves from most other developing countries by the scale and speed with which their economies are developing. China, in particular, proves that capitalism and democracy can develop separately (contrary to the popular theories of Milton Friedman, for example), as China marries capitalism ("with Chinese characteristics") to an economy still dominated by state owned enterprises. Historically, developing countries had little influence in shaping the rules of international trade, but the combination of Brazil, China, and India has changed the dynamic. When they advance common interests in world trade forums, they can influence the practice and the rules that once had been largely dictated by the developed world, particularly Europe and the United States.

Governments do not long like to be dependent on other countries for food, which makes agriculture, and subsidies to agriculture, the most <u>contentious</u> of trade issues. Developing countries have always feared significant job displacement when confronting free trade, and developed countries have long craved access to the populations of developing countries because they are potential consumers of goods known not to be produced in those countries. Developing countries also tend to fear free trade because the availability of goods to buy that they do not produce can only retard or terminate the possibility that they will ever produce them.

An important common characteristic of Brazil, China, and India is that, while they identify themselves as "developing", they generally embrace free trade because they see their paths to prosperity through exports. Nonetheless, India has led the developing world's objections to European and American agricultural subsidies, with the aggressive support of Brazil and China.

1. Which of the following is NOT true about the features of developing countries?
   A. They are developing at different rates.
   B. They fear free markets.
   C. They reach different stages of development.
   D. They have different views of trade.
2. The economic terms of "developing" and "developed" refer to _____.
   A. the construction, maintenance, and operation of infrastructure
   B. the production of increasingly sophisticated goods and services
   C. the opening of markets
   D. All the above.
3. In what way are the developing countries mentioned in the passage different from most other developing countries?
   A. Its rapid and large-scale development in economy.
   B. Its combination of capitalism and democracy.
   C. Its influence in shaping the rules of international trade.
   D. Its economic characteristics.
4. The following words are the synonyms of the word "contentious" in Paragraph 3 EXCEPT _____.
   A. disputatious   B. quarrelsome
   C. agreeable   D. argumentative
5. What do Brazil, China and India share according to the passage?
   A. They welcome free markets.
   B. They are backward because of regionalism.
   C. They are prosperous through exports.
   D. They lead the world's objections to European and American agricultural subsides.

Read the following passage and answer the questions.

The Chinese government has announced that the largest scale processing trade policy contraction plan will be implemented in the next month for less than one month since the implementation of the largest scale export tax refund reduction policy in China. There may be many enterprises stamping their feet about this policy transformation in the Pearl River Delta Region and the Yangtze River Delta Region with the most developed processing trade.

Among the exported goods of high levels, the processing trade enjoys a higher percentage. In 2006, the total amount of computer and telecommunication products export of China has reached 191.001 billion USD, and among them the percentage for trade modes of processing with imported materials and the processing with materials supplied by customers is 91.34%; among the laptop export, the percentage for the trade modes of processing with imported materials and processing with materials supplied by customers among the total export amount is 99.73%. In other words, the optimization of exported good structure among the trade statistics of China is largely attributed to the processing trade. The development of the processing trade has created large amount of employment opportunities for China as well, and currently the direct undertakes involved in the processing trade is approximately 30 million to 40 million people, which is approximately 20% of the total population involved in the second industry in China, and the employment population involved in the relevant supporting industries is approximately 50 million to 60 million people. According to such achievements, we could know that it's no doubt that some scholars praise the processing trade as the new route for industrialization in China.

However, besides the achievements, we shall notice throngs of problems existed in the processing trade of China: the processing trade is basically equal to label production, with low technological content and added-value, so that the total profit amount of the Chinese processing trade link among the entire industrial chain is only around 10%; the foreign-invested enterprises are dominant in the processing trade industry, and the domestic enterprises of China have very few opportunities to participate, and the circumstances are more serious in top end products, and the processing trade is nearly a piece of "flying land" in the entire industrial system of China; the processing trade consumes large amount of lands, energies and resources; the environmental pollution is serious; the most critical point is that some development tendencies of the processing trade apparently want to fix China at the bottom end of the international division industry and unable of saving itself.

1. What plan will come into effect shortly after the export tax refund reduction policy?

   _____.

2. What does the example of 2006 in Paragraph 2 suggest?

   _____.

3. What is the result of the development of processing trade?

   _____.

4. How do some scholars praise the processing trade in China?

_____.

5. Why do China's enterprises have less opportunities to participate in the processing trade?

_____.

8 **Translate the following sentences into Chinese.**

1. Numerous other new laws and regulations covering nearly all aspects of trading with China have been issued or have come into force, all with the purpose of fulfilling China's accession commitments.

_____

_____

2. In the meantime, provincial and local authorities are still reviewing their laws and regulations to see if they are consistent with national laws.

_____

_____

3. Proponents of American foreign assistance describe it as a tool to create new markets for American exporters, to prevent crises and advance democracy and prosperity.

_____

_____

4. Trade barriers remain high, especially in the service and agricultural sectors, where American producers are especially competitive.

_____

_____

5. The governor adheres to the belief that there should be no link between trade policies and labor and environmental standards.

_____

_____

9 **Read and answer the questions raised for this case.**

Case: South Korea

    Years of war devastated South Korea's plant and equipment, but surviving workers carried their skills into the post-war era. For the following decade, the government maintained a protectionist outlook, not only imposing high trade barriers but also maintaining an overvalued exchange rate. Starting in the mid-1960s, Korean leaders shifted the policy mix toward outward orientation. A combination of trade, tax, credit, and exchange-rate incentives gave the Korean economy a pro-export tilt.

During 1961 to 1980, Korean exports grew by almost 24 percent per year in real terms, while the share of exports in Korea's economic output soared from about 5 percent to 33 percent. While the initial phase of industrial development focused on labor-intensive sectors, in the early 1970s Korea moved to a second phase of capital-intensive and technology-intensive production. Today, of course, Korea has become a premier exporter of electronics, machinery, steel, and autos.

But residual protection detracted from overall Korean performance. Data for 38 Korean industries over 1963 to 1983 demonstrate a negative correlation between protection and productivity growth. "The Korean data present evidence that less intervention in trade is linked to higher productivity growth," says economist Jong-Wha Lee of Korea University in Seoul. In fact, plain old special interests better explain the pattern of Korean protection than calculations of economic gain.

What lessons have you learned from the post-war economic experience of South Korea?

 Extended Exercise

Write a short essay of least 120 words following the requirements given below.

1. Give a brief account of import and export.
2. Analyze the reasons.
3. Give suggestions for improving the sales of textile and garment.

2009年1月至11月份纺织品服装进出口数据统计

	1月	2月	3月	4月	5月	6月	7月	8月	9月	10月	11月
出口额(亿美元)	152.3	66.7	121.6	124.9	123	139.9	163.6	157	167.4	146.5	139.6
同比增幅(%)	-3.3	-15.8	-10.3	-10.9	-11.8	-11.75	-12	-12.65	-11.95	-11.9	-11.4
进口额(亿美元)	7.9	10	11.8	13.3	12.4	14.1	14.2	12	13.1	11.9	13.2
同比增幅(%)	-36.7	-18	-16	-15.5	-16.5	-14.3	-13.6	-13.5	-12.2	-12.2	-10.7

Words for reference:

纺织品和服装：textiles and garments

顺　差：surplus

大幅下跌：slum

启动内需：to start domestic demand

Global Market Place

1 Match the following business terms with the Chinese equivalents.

1. Regional Economic Integration
2. The International Trade Commission
3. Central America Free Trade Agreement
4. Caribbean Single Market and Economy
5. The Asia-Pacific Economic Cooperation
6. General Agreement on Tariffs and Trade
7. The ASEAN–China Free Trade Area (ACFTA)

A. 加勒比海国家单一市场和经济体
B. 关贸总协定
C. 中国—东盟自由贸易区
D. 中美洲自由贸易协定
E. 区域经济一体化
F. 亚太经合组织
G. 国际贸易委员会

2 Choose the best answers.

1. Emerging markets include _____.
   A. India
   B. the United States
   C. Japan
   D. France
2. Emerging markets are _____.
   A. regional economic powerhouses
   B. industrialized nations
   C. developed countries
   D. multinationals
3. Emerging markets face the most challenging task of _____.
   A. selling out state-led enterprises
   B. reducing government's intervention
   C. controlling corruption
   D. taking structural reforms
4. Most Central America and the Caribbean _____.
   A. possess rich natural resources
   B. are export-oriented
   C. enjoy excellent infrastructure system
   D. suffered political instability
5. NAFTA was signed among _____.
   A. America, Canada and Cuba
   B. America, Mexico and Cuba
   C. America, Canada and Mexico
   D. Canada, Mexico and Cuba

6. Canada's political stability is threatened by _____.
    A. separatist movement   B. long-standing national conflict
    C. bilingual labeling law   D. two-way trade

7. The least integrative economic integration is _____.
    A. the free trade area   B. the customs union
    C. the economic union   D. the common market

8. The aim of economic integration is to _____.
    A. erect the tariff wall   B. reduce barriers to trade
    C. establish new policies   D. attract foreign investment

9. Economic integration may result in _____.
    A. high production costs   B. small-scale production
    C. lower prices for customers   D. fewer opportunities of investment

•10. Economic integration in Europe is _____.
    A. LAFTA   B. EU
    C. FATT   D. APEC

3 **Complete the following dialogues and practice them with your partner.**

Dialogue ①

> A. customer base   B. sensitive   C. strategies   D. overseas market   E. large-scale production

A: Bob, I went over the sales figures in the market research report. If we take that report and compare it with our survey of customer buying habits, there is only one conclusion.

B: What is it?

A: Our national market becomes increasingly smaller.

B: What do you think we should start to do?

A: To exploit the _____1_____. You know the process of globalization brings us challenges as well as vast opportunities.

B: So what are the detailed strategies?

A: First, we should expand our production. With _____2_____, we can lower per-unit costs.

B: And then?

A: Choose indirect export as the entry mode to the overseas market.

B: You know the overseas market is _____3_____ to price. I suggest we lower the price next step.

A: Absolutely right. Price is vital in the fierce market competition, so we can use it to build our _____4_____. If our customers are attracted by the low price, they will buy and become loyal to our brand. When our customer base is solid on our products, we can bring the price up.

B: That sounds really like a clever strategy.

A: This is a very competitive market. We have got to come up with a few clever _____5_____ to keep our place on top.

Dialogue ②

> A. the demand for the firm's product in China
> B. probably the easiest and quickest way to enter China
> C. a foreign firm must choose an appropriate strategy to enter China market
> D. firms may need to utilize more than one strategy to adequately penetrate the market
> E. probably yields the best overall penetration into China market

A: Many foreign companies want to enter China market for the fast development of economy in China. However, _____6_____. Could you please give me a brief account of this market?

B: OK. There are generally three fundamental strategies: export via Hong Kong distributors, export via direct channels in China, and set up a joint venture.

A: Please go ahead.

B: Market entry via a Hong Kong distributor is _____7_____, but may be the least desirable in terms of overall market penetration.

A: Then what is the second way?

B: Export via direct channels in China is probably more difficult and time consuming than the first one, but it may be better off for a firm's overall penetration.

A: So what about the last strategy?

B: Market entry via a joint venture may be more difficult and time-consuming than the other two strategies just mentioned, but _____8_____. Utilizing this strategy, both sides could gain the most benefit. Besides, China is a huge, fragmented market. Thus, _____9_____.

A: Can all the strategies be counted on?

B: I just name a few. There are a number of other market entry strategies; each strategy has its own advantages and disadvantages. The specific strategy a firm chooses will depend on how the Chinese "view" the foreign firm's entering their market, and _____10_____.

A: Yes, you are absolutely right.

B: In a word, to be successful, companies will need to combine various market entry strategies to fully penetrate the market.

④ **Read the following passages and decide which business term each passage is describing.**

1. FTAA ( )   2. OPEC ( )   3. GATT ( )   4. MFN ( )   5. APEC ( )

A. A cartel comprising 12 leading oil-producing countries that seeks to coordinate oil production and pricing policies. One of the principal goals is the determination of the best means for safeguarding the cartel's interests, individually and collectively. It also pursues ways and means of ensuring the stabilization of prices in international oil markets with a view to eliminating harmful and unnecessary fluctuations.

B. A proposed agreement to eliminate or reduce the trade barriers among all countries in the America but Cuba. In the last round of negotiations, trade ministers from 34 countries met in Miami, Florida, the United States, in November 2003 to discuss the proposal. The proposed agreement was an extension of the North American Free Trade Agreement (NAFTA) between Canada, Mexico and the United States.

C. A forum for 21 Pacific Rim countries to cooperate on regional trade and investment liberalization and facilitation. Its objectives are to enhance the positive gains, to develop and strengthen an open multilateral trading system, and to reduce barriers to trade of goods and services as well as investments.

D. A multilateral trade agreement aimed at expanding international trade as a means of raising world welfare. Its rules reduce uncertainty in connection with commercial transactions across national borders. Ninety-two countries accounting for approximately 80 percent of world trade are contracting parties to it, and some 30 percent additional countries associated with it benefit from the application of its provisions to their trade.

E. A status or level of treatment accorded by one state to another in international trade. The term means the country which is the recipient of this treatment must, nominally, receive equal trade advantages as the "most favored nation" by the country granting such treatment. (Trade advantages include low tariffs or high import quotas.)

⑤ Read the passage and fill in the blanks.

The biggest, fastest-growing economies of the Third World are Brazil, Russia, India, and China. But while the Big Four, also known as BRICs, have ___1___ most investors' attention in recent years, there are also opportunities in less ___2___ but more promising emerging markets ___3___ Indonesia, Vietnam, Turkey and South Africa. Some economists ___4___ that these countries could be the next wave of emerging markets stardom. They have large and young populations, ___5___ economics, relative political stability and ___6___ financial systems. In addition, they are for the most part	1. A. attracted B. absorbed
	   C. assimilated D. stimulated
	2. A. popular B. interesting
	   C. prominent D. useful
	3. A. for example B. as
	   C. as for D. such as
	4. A. declare B. predict
	   C. announce D. promise
	5. A. simple B. various
	   C. different D. diversified
	6. A. awful B. decent
	   C. abnormal D. regular

unhampered by high inflation, trade imbalances or sovereign debt bombs.

Indonesia's demographics, natural resources and ____7____ stable politics have set up the country for ____8____ could be a very strong decade of growth. Its economy doubled in the past five years and in greater Jakarta — the world's second-largest ____9____ area with roughly 23 million people — per-capita GDP grew ____10____ 11 percent each year from 2006 through 2009. More importantly, this growth was ____11____ by the private sector, not by government spending — the private sector ____12____ roughly 90 percent of the country's GDP. Despite this income growth, Indonesia still has the lowest unit labor costs in the Asia-Pacific ____13____. This has attracted manufacturing activities from China. Because half of Indonesia's population is 25 years older or younger, the workforce as a ____14____ of total population will rise over the next 20 years. This should increase the country's consumption levels and ____15____ further economic growth.

Vietnam has seen rapid economic growth in recent years. It also has picked up some manufacturing base ____16____ was formerly in China. The country's per-capita income of $1 050 last year was nearly fivefold higher ____17____ it was in the mid-1990s, and in Hanoi, the income level is closing in on $2 000 per person.

Turkey's economy is dynamic and currently ____18____ by strong underlying trends that point to long-term growth ahead. Its economy is the sixth largest in Europe and in the top 20 worldwide with a 2009 GDP of $615 billion. While Europe ____19____ makes up more than half of Turkey's exports, the current government has ____20____ to increase exports to Middle East trading partners as a hedge against economic volatility in Europe.

7. A. relatively   B. absolutely
    C. especially   D. extremely
8. A. that   B. which
    C. what   D. whom
9. A. rural   B. land
    C. country   D. urban
10. A. to   B. at
    C. by   D. with
11. A. pulled   B. driven
    C. formed   D. raised
12. A. consists of   B. makes in
    C. accounts for   D. comes up
13. A. place   B. block
    C. ground   D. region
14. A. portion   B. ingredient
    C. element   D. segment
15. A. fuel   B. rise
    C. complete   D. achieve
16. A. when   B. whom
    C. what   D. that
17. A. as   B. like
    C. than   D. for
18. A. offered   B. suggested
    C. combined   D. supported
19. A. still   B. also
    C. yet   D. even
20. A. taken steps   B. taken places
    C. given away   D. given up

Read the following passage and choose the best answers.

Policies of openness to foreign direct investment and international trade have enabled countries around the world to leapfrog economically over their neighbors. The historical rise of Hong Kong is one example. Hong Kong's economic strengths can be traced to a combination of factors, including its business-friendly laws and policies, a local population that is culturally oriented to transacting trade and business, and Hong Kong' geographic proximity to the major economies of China, Japan and Taiwan.

In 1997, Hong Kong reverted back to Chinese control. However, free enterprise is governed under the agreement of Basic Law, which established Hong Kong as a separate Special Administrative Region (SAR) of China, under its Basic Law, in force until 2047, Hong Kong will retain its legal, social, economic, and political systems apart from China's. Hong Kong is guaranteed the right to its own monetary system and financial autonomy. And the Hong Kong SAR maintains an independent tax system and the right to free trade.

Hong Kong has an open business structure, which freely encourages foreign direct investment. Any company that wishes to do business here is free to do so as long as it complies with local laws. Hong Kong's legal and institutional framework combined with its good banking and financial facilities and business-friendly tax systems have encouraged foreign direct investment as many multinationals located their regional headquarters in Hong Kong.

According to a 2000 government survey, 570 U.S. companies, and 236 British companies have their regional headquarters in Hong Kong. The late 1980s and the early to mid-1990s were especially prosperous times in Hong Kong as many of these international companies set up regional headquarters. Businesses scrambled for office space, and apartment prices skyrocketed. It was not uncommon during this period for brand-new residential buildings suddenly to be demolished and replaced with even taller structures following changes in zoning regulations.

Because of the shift in production to the mainland of China and other Asian countries or districts, there is not much manufacturing left in Hong Kong. What remains is light in nature and veers toward high-value-added products. In fact, 80 percent of Hong Kong's gross domestic product now comes from its high-value-added service sector.

Chinese cultural influences have always affected business and are increasingly so today. Many pundits claim that Hong Kong already resembles China's free-trade zone. And, indeed, the two economies are becoming increasingly intertwined. As a result of common culture and geography, Hong Kong entrepreneurs often act as brokers and intermediaries for companies around the world that want to do business with the mainland of China. Accordingly, Hong Kong has thrived as an entrepot for the main land of China, receiving goods from it and preparing the goods for shipment to the rest of the world, and vice versa.

1. _____ contribute to Hong Kong's fast-growing economic development.

   A. Its business-friendly policies

    B. The local population

    C. Its geography

    D. All of the above.

2. As a separate Special Administrative Region of China, Hong Kong _____.

    A. is absolutely independent of Chinese laws

    B. will retain its legal, economic, and political systems apart from China's forever

    C. is guaranteed the right to its own financial autonomy under the Basic Law

    D. maintains an independent tax system and the right to free trade at any time

3. Which of the following is NOT mentioned as an attraction for foreign direct investment in Hong Kong?

    A. Its legal system.

    B. Its cultural system.

    C. Its financial system.

    D. Its tax system.

4. In the late 1980s and the early to mid-1990s, _____.

    A. Hong Kong's economy was unprecedentedly prosperous

    B. 236 British companies had their regional headquarters in Hong Kong

    C. few residential buildings were replaced with even taller structures

    D. Chinese cultural influences began to affect business in Hong Kong

5. We can infer from the passage that _____.

    A. there is still much manufacturing left in Hong Kong

    B. Hong Kong emphasizes development of labor-intensive industries

    C. any company that does business in Hong Kong complies with the local laws

    D. Hong Kong acts as a bridge between the mainland of China and global corporations

7 Read the following passage and answer the questions.

Integration increases market size and therefore may result in a lower degree of monopoly in the production of certain goods and services. This is because a larger market will tend to increase the number of competing firms, resulting in greater efficiency and lower prices for consumers.

Many industries, such as steel and automobiles, require large-scale production in order to obtain economies of scale in production. Therefore, certain industries may simply not be economically viable in smaller, trade-protected countries. However, the formation of a trading bloc enlarges the market so that large-scale production is justified. The lower per-unit production costs scale economies may then be obtained. These lower production costs resulting from greater production for an enlarged market are called internal economies of scale. This is evident if the region adopts common standards, thus shaping bigger markets for the companies and enabling them to become global powerhouses.

In a common market, external economies of scale may also be present. Because a common market allows factors of production to flow freely across borders, the firm may now have access to cheaper capital, more highly skilled labor, or superior technology. These factors will improve the quality of the firm's goods or services or will lower costs or both.

When factors of production are freely mobile, the wealth of the common market countries, in aggregate, will likely increase. The theory behind this contention is straightforward: factor mobility will lead to the movement of labor and capital from areas of low productivity to areas of high productivity. In addition to the economic gains from factor mobility, there are other benefits not so easily quantified. The free movement of labor fosters a higher level of communication across cultures. This, in turn, leads to a higher degree of cross-cultural understanding; as people move, their ideas, skills, and ethnicity move with them.

Again, however, <u>factor mobility will not necessarily benefit each country in the common market</u>. A poorer country, for example, may lose badly needed investment capital to a richer country, where opportunities are perceived to be more profitable. Another disadvantage of factor mobility that is often cited is the brain-drain phenomenon. A poorer country may loose its most talented workers when they are free to search out better opportunities. More-developed member countries worry that companies may leave for other member countries where costs of operation, such as social costs, are lower.

1. What is the result of the increasing number of competing firms in a large market?

   _____.

2. What are the internal economies of scale?

   _____.

3. Why may external economies be present in a common market?

   _____.

4. What benefits can the common market countries get from factor mobility?

   _____.

5. Why does the author say "factor mobility will not necessarily benefit each country in the common market"?

   _____.

8 Translate the following sentences into Chinese.

1. Learning from the experience of pioneering companies in emerging markets, investors know they have to contend with a minefield of competing local interests, overloaded infrastructure, difficulties in retaining skilled people, tortuous supply chains, unfamiliar local HR practices and communication barriers.

   _____

   _____

2. These difficulties in exploiting scale economies reduce the gap between multinationals operating in China and Chinese enterprises that typically start from a strong base in a geographically limited provincial or local market.

   _____

   _____

3. Global market has its own set of economic rules — rules that revolve around opening, deregulating and privatizing your economy in order to make it more competitive and attractive to foreign investment.

   _____

   _____

4. Despite optimism about future prospects throughout East Asia and Latin America, the markets that will account for the overwhelming incremental growth in world imports can be narrowed down to fewer than a dozen, which we called "The Big Emerging Markets."

   _____

   _____

5. Important as Europe is to America as a market, and also as a competitor, we must also understand its vital importance to us as a force for opening global markets and shaping the global economic structure.

   _____

   _____

 Read and answer the questions raised for the case.

Case: Russia's Economic Transition

Facts: Throughout the presidencies of Boris Yeltsin in the 1990s and today that of Vladimir Putin, Russia has opened its doors to international trade, investment, tourism, and the media. In sharp contrast of the Soviet Union, Russia now publishes voluminous economic, social and demographic information.

Since 1991, Russia's real GDP growth rate has been more than twice the underweighted average of the other G-8 members. During Putin's tenure since 2000, the number of Russia's privately owned enterprises more than doubled, to nearly 80 percent of all enterprises, while the share of state-owned enterprises shrank from 14 percent to less than 4 percent.

However, despite the fast development of economy, inflation continues to hover around 10 percent, and capital flight was more than nine billion U.S. dollars in 2007. Furthermore, the process of privatization usually involves bribing government officials — which makes many international companies nervous.

Questions: Where is the Russian economy heading? Toward decentralized resource allocation by competitive markets, or backward toward decision-making by the state and its bureaucracies? The answer remains highly uncertain. In your opinion, what is the implication of this phenomenon?

 Extended Exercise

Study the following two graphs carefully and write an essay in no less than 120 words. Your essay should cover all the information provided and meet the requirements below:

1. Interpret the following graphs.
2. State why China can maintain the stability of RMB and give your comments.

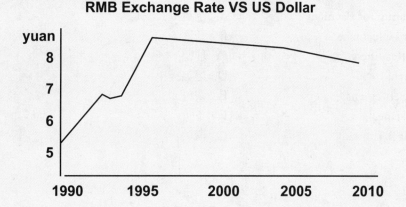

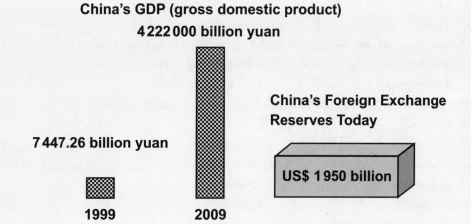

Trade Procedure

① Match the following terms with the Chinese equivalents.

1. Negotiating for Payment   A. 空运单
2. Customs Clearance   B. 开证
3. Cargo Readiness   C. 理赔
4. Air Waybill   D. 记名提单
5. Claim Settlement   E. 议付
6. L/C issuance   F. 备货
7. Straight B/L   G. 清关

② Choose the best answers.

1. You usually cannot obtain information about potential customers through _____.

   A. a bank   B. a chamber of commerce

   C. a consul   D. an underwriter

2. Which one of the following parties is NOT involved in L/C application?

   A. The importer.   B. The issuing bank.

   C. The exporter.   D. The opening bank.

3. Which of the following products does NOT need an export license?

   A. Coal.   B. Uranium.

   C. Petroleum.   D. Digital cameras.

4. The following are all part of trade negotiation EXCEPT _____.

   A. enquiry   B. offer

   C. acceptance   D. quotation

5. Which one of the following statements is TRUE?

   A. Shipment should be effected before the L/C is received.

   B. Shipment should be effected after the L/C is received.

C. Shipment should be effected when the L/C is received.

D. None of the above.

6. Which link in trade procedure is basic to the development of an industrial society?

   A. Negotiation.   B. Payment.

   C. Insurance.   D. Transportation.

7. After receiving the L/C, against which document should the exporter examine the L/C?

   A. The bill of exchange.   B. The sales contract.

   C. The export license.   D. The commercial invoice.

8. Which of the following is NOT an advantage of ocean transportation?

   A. Rapidness.   B. Lower freight.

   C. Larger loading capacity.   D. Regular voyages.

9. Under CFR terms, what document should the exporter send to the importer after effecting the shipment?

   A. The shipping instructions. B. The shipping advice.

   C. The insurance policy.   D. The bill of lading.

10. The following are all correct about the bill of lading EXCEPT _____.

    A. it is a contract of carriage.

    B. it is a cargo receipt.

    C. It is a document of title to the goods.

    D. it is the general description of the quality and quantity of the goods.

③ Complete the following dialogues and practice them with your partner.

Dialogue ①

A. customs formalities   B. top priority   C. retailing   D. committed   E. capacity

A: Mr. Zhang I wonder if it is possible for you to effect shipment during March, Mr. Zhang?

B: I don't think we can make it.

A: Then when can we expect the shipment at the earliest?

B: By the middle of April. That's the best we can do.

A: It's too late. You see, May is the season for this commodity in our market, and we have to find someone else to do the _____1_____. What's more, our _____2_____ are rather complicated. All this will take us at least a couple of weeks.

B: I quite see your point. But the factories are fully _____3_____. In fact, many of our clients are placing orders for delivery in the second quarter.

A: This may be so. But could you find some way to rearrange the schedule and make our order your _____4_____? There is no harm trying, I suppose. You see, a timely delivery means a lot to us.

B: But we have done our utmost in the matter, Mr. Willis We have been keeping in constant touch with our manufacturers. We check up on their production schedule almost every day as against our orders. As new orders are pouring in, they are working at full _____5_____. The best we can promise is to deliver the goods 4 or 5 days earlier.

A: Well, in that case, I think I must take things as they are.

B: OK, we'll do our best to advance the shipment anyhow.

Dialogue ②

A. lose our goodwill and future business

B. stowage on board, weather effects, storage in the warehouse

C. lodge a claim with your company

D. raised together with the conclusive evidence immediately after arrival of the goods at the destination

E. adopt rigid processing controls and maintain an adequate packing process

A: I'm sorry Mr. Hu, I have to _____6_____. It's a most unpleasant incident.

B: What's up?

A: It's about the 1 000 cases of dried seafood. Many bags have been found blown. Our Health Authorities said that they were no longer suitable for human consumption.

B: I'm awfully sorry to hear that. But I'm rather surprised because our plant has always given due care to the selection of raw materials. They _____7_____. Each bag is examined before leaving the plant.

A: Our surveyors just stated that inferior raw materials and inadequate packing are the causes of the blown bags.

B: As our long-term customer, you perhaps know well that the Chinese Commodity Inspection Bureau exercises a strict inspection on the goods before shipment.

A: I hold your Inspection Bureau in good esteem. But casual mishaps might be possible.

B: I think, in an incident like this, we have to take other factors into account, such as, _____8_____, etc.

A: Our surveyors said nothing of such possibilities. I have brought with me several bags drawn at random from this shipment. We do hope you would indemnify us for the loss in some way or other.

B: According to the contract, claims, if any, must be _____9_____. The goods reached you in June. We are now in October. Why didn't you file a claim immediately after you found the blown bags?

A: You see, Mr. Hu, the market was stagnant when the goods arrived. We couldn't sell the goods in a dull season. So we have to put them in storage. It was not until September that the blown bags were discovered.

B: Well now. That's where the shoe pinches. Since you stored up the goods in such hot weather, even the best bagged goods might get blown.

A: Anyhow, if the goods were in perfectly sound condition, they could not have become deteriorated in such a short time. Our buyers have complained a lot. If the matter is further delayed, we might _____10_____. As the sole dealer promoting your products in our market, you won't see our position weakened, will you?

B: You're right. Since our relations have always been amicable, we'll do our best to help you out of the trouble. I suggest that you tell us the exact number of the blown bags and send us another survey report in detail for our consideration.

A: Thank you very much. But what do you want us to do with the blown bags? We'd rather have them replaced.

B: Please keep them until we give you a definite reply.

A: Well, I'll email back immediately and ask my people to send you the survey report.

④ Read the following passages and decide which document each passage is describing.

1. Draft ( )	2. B/L ( )	3. L/C ( )
4. Invoice ( )	5. Packing List ( )	

A. It is the general description of the quality and quantity of the goods and the unit and total price. It constitutes the basis on which other documents are to be prepared.

B. It gives information such as the number, date, name and description of the goods, shipping marks, packing, number of packages, specific contents of each package, its net weight and gross weight, etc.

C. It serves as a cargo receipt signed by the carrier and issued to the shipper or consignor, constitutes a contract of carriage between the carrier and the consignor and is a document of title to the goods, and the legal holder of it is the owner of the goods it covers.

D. Its unique feature is bilateral security, which means it offers security to both the seller and the buyer. The former has the security to get paid provided he presents impeccable documents while the latter has the security to get the goods required through the documents he stipulates in it.

E. It is an unconditional order to a bank or a customer to pay a sum of money to someone on demand or at a fixed time in the future.

5 Read the passage and fill in the blanks.

Transportation is one of the basic ___1___ in trade procedure. It permits the specialization of work effort necessary to achieve ___2___ and productivity. Products must be moved to the locations ___3___ they are needed and wanted, such as ___4___ moved to supermarket. And people, in turn, must use some form of movement to get to the ___5___ to buy the groceries they want and need.

Transportation plays a major role ___6___ the production process. It allows the entrepreneur to assemble more easily the raw ___7___ and labor inputs needed to make a specific product. The same transportation system moves ___8___ products to other producers for subsequent use in their production process, and it moves finished products to ___9___.

As a society, we enjoy a richer and more leisurely life than we would if small communities had to be totally self-sufficient. Transportation has also allowed us ___10___ with countries throughout the world; and this commercial intercourse has helped to eliminate many ___11___ between nations.

In choosing a transportation mode for a particular ___12___, shippers consider as many as six criteria: speed, frequency, dependability, capability, availability and cost. Thus if a shipper seeks ___13___, air and truck are the prime contenders. If the goal is ___14___, then water and pipeline are the prime contenders. Shippers are increasingly combining two or more transportation modes, thanks ___15___ containerization. Containerization consists ___16___ putting the goods in boxes or trailers that are easy to

1. A. concepts   B. ideas
    C. links   D. feudal
2. A. inefficiency   B. efficiency
    C. proficiency   D. probability
3. A. where   B. there
    C. which   D. that
4. A. customers   B. passengers
    C. people   D. groceries
5. A. boutique
    B. department store
    C. supermarket
    D. plaza
6. A. in   B. in
    C. for   D. to
7. A. material   B. stuff
    C. goods   D. cargo
8. A. immediate   B. mediate
    C. finished   D. intermediate
9. A. producers   B. consumers
    C. managers   D. brokers
10. A. trading   B. to have traded
    C. in trading   D. to trade
11. A. friendship   B. barriers
    C. benefits   D. profit
12. A. cargo   B. goods
    C. product   D. coverage
13. A. safety   B. profit
    C. speed   D. value
14. A. high efficiency
    B. small quantity
    C. convenience
    D. low cost
15. A. to   B. for
    C. of   D. with
16. A. in   B. with
    C. of   D. on

transfer ___17___ two transportation modes. Each coordinated mode of transportation offers specific advantages to the shipper. For example, piggyback is cheaper than trucking alone and yet provides flexibility and convenience.

    Transportation decisions must consider the advantages and ___18___ of the various transportation modes and their implications ___19___ other distribution elements such as warehousing and inventory. As the relative costs of different transportation modes change ___20___ time, companies need to reanalyze their options in the search for optimal arrangement.

17. A. during   B. between
    C. in   D. with
18. A. merits   B. features
    C. drawbacks   D. edge
19. A. in   B. on
    C. to   D. for
20. A. in   B. on
    C. during   D. over

 Read the following passage and complete the sentences.

    Transportation insurance, like all forms of insurance, conforms to certain basic principles. When firms seek cover for goods and units of carriage, they must follow these principles.

    Insurable interest holds that no one may insure anything unless he has an interest in it, which means that if the thing insured is preserved he will derive a benefit from its preservation, but if it is in any way damaged or lost the assured will be adversely affected. Every contract of insurance requires an insurable interest to support it. The time of an event may be crucial to the question of insurable interest. The interest passes with the documents. In cargo insurance we know who has an interest in the cargo at any particular point of time, if we know the sales terms which have been arranged. We can work out who will suffer loss by discovering at what point the property passes from one person to another. The person who is going to suffer the loss is the one who has the insurable interest at any moment.

    Utmost good faith is a very important principle. The people who decide what premium is fair for a particular cover do so on the basis of written statements made in a proposal form. If this statement is untrue, then the premium agreed on will not be a fair one. Suppose one says that a crate contains copper, when in fact it contains gold. The premium required to cover the cheaper metal will be an unfair premium for the more valuable one. The mis-statement is a fraud, and the policy is voidable by the party who is misled. Even if the mis-statement was unintentional, the underwriter would still be deceived and the policy voidable.

Indemnity holds that a contract of insurance is one which restores a person who suffered a loss into the same position as he was in before the loss occurred — not into a better position. Cargo policies are often issued for an agreed value and are therefore called "valued" policies. The idea is that the compensation payable will be at an agreed figure, often at invoiced cost plus freight and forwarding charges plus the insurance premium plus an agreed percentage such as 10 percent. This represents a profit that could have been earned on the capital tied up in the transaction.

Questions: Fill in the blanks with what you learned from the passage.

1. The principles of insurance covered in this passage are _____, _____, and _____.

2. In cargo insurance we know who has an interest in the cargo at any particular point of time, if _____.

3. In cargo insurance, we can figure out who will suffer loss by _____.

4. The principle of indemnity holds that the purpose of a contract of insurance is to _____.

5. Usually the insured amount is 100% plus 10% of the invoice value. The additional 10% represents _____.

7 Read the following passage and decide which statement is True (T) or False (F).

Packaging for exporting requires a different focus than packaging for domestic use. Often domestic packaging is primarily designed to display the product for sale, save weight, or advertise the shipper's company. Export packaging is primarily designed to protect the product from the hazards of international shipment and to comply with legal requirements.

What packaging is best for exported products depends on the nature and value of the goods, the type of transportation involved, and the legal requirements. The first rule to be observed when packaging for export is to consider the entire journey, including the short hauls to and from the primary carriers. Pack the goods so that they will survive each leg of the trip intact.

Wooden crates are made with a strong wooden frame. Wooden boards, called skids, are often nailed to the bottom of a crate to hold it off the floor, preventing water damage and making it possible to handle the crate with a forklift truck. Plastic sheeting or water-repellant coated paper may be placed on the exterior or used as an interior wrapping for the cargo to make the package resistant to water damage. In order to prevent the crate from coming apart, the entire crate may be bound with wire or strapping for additional strength.

Cargo such as grain, cement, and granular chemicals are often shipped in paper sacks or cloth bags. Such cargo may be placed on wooden pallets or loaded with a cargo net. Many of these cargos are susceptible to water damage, so such cargo should not be stored directly on the floor if the floor could be a source of moisture.

Some materials, such as large bundles of fibers or other raw materials, may be shipped as bales. Bales are usually wrapped in burlap on the outside and may have waterproof inner wrap as the protection. Bales are usually held together with steel strapping.

Drums, casks, or kegs are all names for cylindrical fiberboard, plastic, wood, or metal containers. The metal ones are usually designed for liquid cargo. Fiberboard and plastic drums are suitable for powdered cargo. They often have a fitted metal or plastic strap around the top that secures the top.

Some cargo requires special handling. A number of international pictorial markings are available to advise handlers that a certain crate must, for instance, be protected from heat or freezing or not be handled with hooks. These markings should be made on the package indelibly because damage could be done if they are rubbed off. Stenciling with good ink is often the preferred method.

Finally, it is a temptation to proudly advertise the content of the container on the side and place one's company logo prominently on the shipment. Often this practice is good advertising domestically, but internationally it only notifies pilferers what booty is to be had inside. Smart shippers use blind marks that usually consist of coded strings of letters and numbers to identify the shipment.

1. The domestic packaging is for sales promotion. (   )
2. The export packaging is to make the goods more attractive. (   )
3. The main function of skids is to protect the crates from coming apart. (   )
4. The plastic sheeting in the exterior of a crate is used for the purpose of anti-moisture. (   )
5. The shipping marks on the goods can warn the porters at the harbor against rough handling.(   )

8 Translate the following sentences into Chinese.

1. Proposal forms are not customary in cargo insurance, but many firms do use a transit application form which lists the information they require.

_____

_____

2. The existence of a letter of credit assures payment to the beneficiary if the terms and conditions of the letter of credit are fulfilled.

_____

_____

3. The quality and quantity of merchandise shipped, although specified in the documents submitted to the bank as required by the L/C terms, ultimately depends on the honesty and integrity of the seller who has manufactured, packaged, and arranged for shipment of the merchandise.

_____

_____

4. A straight bill of lading is made out so that only the named consignee is entitled to take delivery of the goods under the bill.

_____

_____

5. When goods are shipped on a non-commercial basis, such as samples or exhibits, or when the goods are extremely valuable, a straight bill of lading is generally issued.

_____

_____

9 **Read and answer the questions raised for the case.**

Case: Who is Responsible?

Company A consigns 10 000 bags of coffee beans to a shipping company B and requires the latter to ship the goods from Shanghai to Bangkok. The captain issues the clean B/L upon receipt and examination of the goods, stating that the goods are in apparent good condition. However, when the goods reach the destination, the consignee in Thailand, Company C, finds there are 600 bags short-weighted by 25%. Company C then files a claim against the shipping company B for compensation. Shipping company B declares that they have not examined the goods bag by bag, but they have solid evidence that Company A should be kept liable for the loss.

Question: Who should compensate Company C?

10 **Extended Exercise**

Write a letter based on the following situation.

Suppose you have concluded a business of woolen carpets with Mr. Finch. But upon taking delivery of the goods, you find 11 cartons are broken and the carpets in them soiled. You are writing to lodge a claim with Mr. Finch. Indicating that the loss is caused by improper packing, you request that Mr. Finch grant you a 15% discount. Otherwise, you will ask for replacement for the whole lot of goods.

Business Contract

1 Match the following contract expressions with the Chinese equivalents.

1. Original of the Contract
2. Alternation of the Contract
3. Performance of the Contract
4. Contractual Obligation
5. Expiration of Contract
6. Contract of Arbitration
7. Termination of the Contract

A. 履行合同
B. 合同期满
C. 合同正本
D. 仲裁合同
E. 解除合同
F. 修改合同
G. 合同义务

2 Choose the best answers.

1. The Sellers shall effect insurance for 110% of the invoice value against All Risks and War Risk _____ the relevant Ocean Marine Cargo Clauses of the People's Insurance Company of China.
   A. with
   B. of
   C. as of
   D. as per

2. This contract enters into force upon _____ for a period of two whole years.
   A. recognition
   B. signature
   C. consent
   D. acceptance

3. During the period of this Contract, both Parties should strictly _____ the terms and conditions of this contract.
   A. abide of
   B. abide with
   C. abide by
   D. abide in

4. This Agreement is _____ in quadruplicate, each party holding two copies.
   A. made out
   B. made on
   C. made into
   D. made off

5. In the event of any breach of the terms by one party, the other party _____ to claim the termination of this Agreement.

    A. to entitle   B. be entitled

    C. is entitled   D. entitles

6. According to the Agreement stipulated by us, the shipment time is April or May at our _____ and the goods will be shipped in one _____.

    A. choice; shipment   B. option; lot

    C. decision; cargo   D. option; consignment

7. Documentary Collection is to be made with the documents to be _____ to the draft.

    A. enclosed   B. attached

    C. given   D. carried

8. This contract is _____ concluded through consultation between the Service Co., Hangzhou and ABC Co., Hong Kong in respect of engagement of Chinese employees.

    A. hereby   B. thereby

    C. hereon   D. thereof

9. We wish to stress that shipment must be made within the time limit prescribed in the contract, as a further _____ will not be considered by our end-users.

    A. prolong   B. protract

    C. expansion   D. extension

10. The contract must be renewed one week _____ their expiration.

    A. on   B. against

    C. for   D. before

③ Complete the following dialogues and practice them with your partner.

A. I have to remind you that our terms are C.I.F London port

B. Your fairness in business dealings is really unsurpassed

C. You have probably been advised of the serious damage done to the last consignment

D. remains that this has made it necessary for us to file a claim on you

E. what were the exact causes of the leakage

Dialogue ①

Palmer: Well, now, Mr. Tang, if you don't mind, I'll talk shop with you directly.

  Tang: All right. In fact, you wish to take up the subject of the Arbutus, don't you?

Palmer: That's right. _____1_____ of 60 cases of Arbutus. Upon its arrival, it was found that about 50% of the cases were leaking, which was regretfully against our contract.

  Tang: Just a minute, Mr. Palmer. Have your people in London discovered _____2_____?

Palmer: I am sorry that it was definitely damaged prior to loading. You may think it a singular case, yet the fact _____3_____.

Tang: As I have said before, the whole business is most unfortunate. We have never come across such a case of damage during loading.

Palmer: _____4_____, according to our contract. While we have full confidence in your Commodities Inspection Bureau in its capacity of quality inspection, this is a case which occurred after their sampling and analysis at the works. I am sure you will think it fair on our part when we suggest that the total value of the parcel should be reduced by 50% and that you should give us an allowance by way of credit for the amount to be set against our future purchases of canned fruits from you.

Tang: To be fair to your company, I am directed by my Shanghai Branch to settle this issue with you amicably on condition that you give us a certificate issued by your Health Department. Now that this is available, I think everything will be in order.

Palmer: I am so glad to hear of your ready agreement. _____5_____. Shall we send you a letter confirming this?

Tang: As soon as you send us a letter confirming this conversation, we'll send you a reply immediately.

Palmer: Thanks ever so much for your cooperation, Mr. Tang. Goodbye.

Tang: Goodbye.

Dialogue ②

A. penalty	B. transaction process	C. anticipated
D. prescribe	E. disturbances	

A: Miss Li, may I ask some questions about the clauses of sales contract?

B: Certainly, we know that a sales contract includes a series of clauses to stipulate both parties' rights and obligations.

A: According to the terms, when damages to goods occur during the _____6_____, the sellers shall take the responsibilities of compensating for the buyers. But what about the Force Majeure? In this case, how about the compensation of damages?

B: Force Majeure refers to the event that can be neither _____7_____ nor reduced to control, for example, an industrial strike that leads to loss of profits. This kind of event enables a seller to avoid his contractual obligations without paying any compensation or_____8_____ to the buyer.

A: So that means the obligations of compensating can be totally omitted if Force Majeure does happen.

B: Yes, in the contract, usually the Force Majeure clause will clearly_____9_____that the buyers are free from such obligations under the circumstances.

A: Then what are the circumstances of Force Majeure?

B: They are commonly in relation to natural disasters such as fire, flood, storm, heavy snow and so on, or those social _____10_____ like war, strike, sanctions and so on.

A: Oh, I know. Thank you, Miss Li.

B: You are welcome.

④ Read the following passages and decide which contract clause each paragraph is describing.

> 1. Clause of Shipment (   )   2. Clause of Price (   )   3. Clause of Claim (   )
> 4. Clause of Force Majeure (   )   5. Clause of Arbitration (   )

A. This clause refers to a means of settling disputes between two parties through the medium of a third party who is not partial to either of the parties to the dispute, and whose decision on the dispute is final and binding, that is, neither party shall bring an appeal for revision before a law court or any other organizations.

B. This clause includes price and total amount. A unit price is composed of four parts: currency unit, unit price figure, measurement unit and delivery terms.

C. When negotiating a transaction, the trading parties should reach an agreement on time of shipment, port of shipment and port of destination, shipping advice, partial shipment and transshipment, dispatch and demurrage, etc. and specify them in the sales contract.

D. This clause refers to the case in which goods may have been damaged during transport and some measures to recover the losses should be taken. The measure can be taken in the following ways: making refund and compensating for other direct losses or expenses; selling the goods at lower prices; or replacing the faulty goods with perfect ones.

E. Under this clause, if the shipment of the contracted goods is prevented or delayed in whole or in part by reason of war, earthquake, flood, fire, storm or other causes which can be neither anticipated nor reduced to control, the seller shall not be liable for non-shipment or late shipment of the goods or non-performance of this contract.

⑤ Read the passage and fill in the blanks.

A contract is an agreement which sets _____1_____ binding obligations of the relevant parties. It is enforceable by law, and any party that fails to _____2_____ his contractual obligations may be sued and forced to make compensation, though most contracts do not _____3_____ disputes.	1. A. forth C. back 2. A. complete C. achieve 3. A. avoid C. give rise to	B. aside D. down B. obey D. fulfill B. comprise D. result from

The contract is based on agreement, which is the result of business negotiations. There are two types of business negotiations: oral and written. The former refers to direct discussions conducted ____4____ trade fairs or by sending trade groups abroad or by inviting foreign customers.

Written negotiations often begin with ____5____ made by the buyers to get information about the goods to be ordered such as quantity, specifications, prices, time of shipment and other terms. An enquiry is made ____6____ engagement on the part of the enquirer. ____7____ a first enquiry, that is, an enquiry sent to an exporter whom the importer has never ____8____, information should be given in the enquiry as to how the name and address of the exporter have been ____9____, the business line and usual practice of the importer, etc. so as to ____10____ the exporter's work.

In response to an enquiry, a ____11____ may be sent by the exporter which should include all the necessary information required by the enquiry. Sometimes, the exporter may make an offer to the time of shipment and the ____12____ of payment desired in addition to an exact description of the goods including the quantity, quality, specifications, packing, etc. The ____13____ period is indispensable ____14____ a firm offer. An offer is considered open until after a stipulated time or until it is accepted or rejected. The offeree may find part of the offer ____15____ and may ask for further discussions of his own proposals which constitute a counter-offer. A counter-offer may be made ____16____ the price, terms of payment, time of shipment or other terms and conditions of the offer. It is a ____17____ of the offer which

4. A. in   B. at
   C. by   D. through
5. A. enquiries   B. offers
   C. counter-offers D. acceptance
6. A. by   B. with
   C. towards   D. without
7. A. On   B. In case of
   C. As if   D. As though
8. A. encountered B. dealt with
   C. run into   D. met with
9. A. rendered   B. received
   C. authorized   D. obtained
10. A. speed up   B. facilitate
    C. enhance   D. stabilize
11. A. quotation B. shipping advice
    C. notice   D. list
12. A. way   B. track
    C. avenue   D. mode
13. A. expiration B. validity
    C. effectiveness D. use-by
14. A. with   B. as
    C. to   D. for
15. A. acceptable B. satisfied
    C. unacceptable D. pleasant
16. A. in terms of B. in relation to
    C. as of   D. so far as
17. A. affirmation B. improvement
    C. refusal   D. evasion

will be invalid and unbinding once a counter-offer is made. The counter-offer thus becomes a new offer made by the original offeree to the original offerer.

Transaction is considered ____18____ once an offer or a counter-offer is accepted. A written contract is generally prepared and signed as the proof of the agreement and as the basis for its execution. When the contract is made by the seller, it is called a sales contract, and when made by the buyer, a ____19____ contract. A sales or purchase confirmation is less detailed than a contract, covering only the essential ____20____ of the transaction. It is usually used for smaller deals or between familiar trade partners.

18. A. fulfilled   B. concluded
    C. excellent   D. integrated
19. A. purchase   B. subcontracting
    C. insurance   D. sales
20. A. tips   B. frames
    C. terms   D. points

6 Read the following passage and decide which statements are true (T) or false (F).

Under consignment, the consignor sends the goods to a foreign consignee who will sell the goods for the consignor according to the agreed terms. The essence of consignment trading is that goods exported on the consignment remain the property to the exporter. Therefore, consignment exports are not really exports because the exporter retains title to the goods until the importer sells the goods to final customers or third parties. So, the exporter is not paid until the goods are sold in the overseas marketplace.

Consignment is rarely used between independent exporters and importers. There is too much risk for the exporters because they are not paid until all goods are sold in the foreign market. This may turn out to be a long period of time. Also, if the goods do not sell well on the foreign market, the exporter may have to get the goods back at his expense or sell the goods on discount. Moreover, most exporters feel that when an importer has his or her money tied up in inventory, he or she will make a greater sales effort. However, importers like consignment because it reduces their risk and requires no additional working capital.

Nonetheless, when the exporter wants to introduce goods to a foreign market, a consignment arrangement might be necessary to encourage the importer to handle the new merchandise. Furthermore, if the exporter wishes to control the foreign market price of his product, he can do so under a consignment contract.

The following is a sample consignment contract.

This Agreement is entered into between ABC Co. (hereinafter referred to as the Consignor), having its registered office in Shanghai, China and XYZ Co. (hereinafter referred to as the Consignee), having its registered office in Beijing, on the following terms and conditions:

1) The Consignor shall from time to time ship laptops to the consignee on Consignment basis at the prevailing international market prices on CIF terms. The interval between each shipment shall be approximately ninety days.

2) The Consignee must try to sell the consignments at the best possible prices after obtaining the approval of the Consignor as to price, terms, etc.

3) Each shipment by ship at the initial stage will not exceed USD200 and the outstanding liabilities on the Consignee shall be in the vicinity of not more than USD100 only.

4) The Consignor shall at no time be responsible for any bad debts arising out of credit sales to any buyers. Making payments to the Consignor shall at all times be the sole responsibility of the Consignee.

5) The Consignee shall accept the Bills of Exchange drawn by the Consignor on him at 90 days' sight with interest payable at 5% per annum.

6) The Consignee shall collect the shipping documents including B/L from the Consignor's bank against Trust Receipt duly signed by the Consignee.

7) The Consignor shall absorb insurance premium and warehousing charges up to the date of delivery to customers.

8) This Agreement is written in English, in two originals; each Party retains one copy.

1. In consignment exports, the title of goods still belongs to the exporter rather than the consignee before the consignee sells the goods to the final customers or third parties. (   )
2. It is favorable to importers to sign contracts with the consignees because the means of consignment can reduce their risks and require little additional capital. (   )
3. According to the clauses in the sample contract, the consignee can sell the consigned goods at the prices of their own will. (   )
4. It is the consignor's obligation to take the responsibilities for bad debts due to credit sales. (   )
5. Insurance premium and warehousing charges should be absorbed by the consignees before the goods are sold. (   )

 Read the following passage and answer the questions.

In today's international business, many agents are active in all kinds of transactions. And therefore, signing agency contracts becomes a necessity in agency business. The following sample exclusive agency agreement includes most of the major clauses.

Exclusive Agency Agreement

This agreement is made and entered into by and between the parties concerned on 5th , September in Dalian, China on the basis of equality and mutual benefit to develop business on terms and conditions mutually agreed upon as follows:

1) The Parties Concerned

Party A: Little Duck Washing Machines Company

Party B: Shangdong Everbright Sales Agency

2) Appointment

Party A hereby appoints Party B as its Exclusive Agent to solicit orders for the commodity stipulated in Article 3 from customers in the territory stipulated in Article 4, and Party B accepts and assumes such appointment.

3) Commodity

"Purple Flower" Brand Washing Machines

4) Territory

In China only

5) Minimum turnover

Party B shall undertake to solicit orders for the above commodity from customers in the above territory during the effective period of this agreement for not less than USD1 000 000.

6) Price and Payment

The price for each individual transaction shall be fixed through negotiations between Party B and the buyer, and subject to Party A's final confirmation. Payment shall be made by confirmed, irrevocable L/C opened by the buyer in favor of Party A, which shall reach Party A 15 days before the date of shipment.

7) Exclusive Right

In consideration of the exclusive rights granted herein, Party A shall not, directly or indirectly, sell or export the commodity stipulated in Article 3 to customers in China through channels other than Party B; Party B shall not sell, distribute or promote the sales of any products competitive with or similar to the above commodity in China and shall not solicit or accept orders for the purpose of selling them outside China. Party A shall refer to Party B any enquiries or orders for the commodity in question received by Party A from other firms in China during the validity of this agreement.

8) Reports on Market Conditions

Party B shall have the obligation to forward once every three months to Party A detailed reports on current market conditions and on consumers' comments. For Party A's reference, Party B shall, from time to time, forward to Party A samples of similar commodity offered by other suppliers, together with their copies, sales position and advertising materials.

9) Commission

Party A shall pay Party B a commission of 5% on the net invoiced selling price on all orders directly obtained by Party B and accepted by Party A. No commission shall be paid until Party A receives the full payment for each order.

10) Termination

During the validity of this agreement, if either of the two parties is found to have violated the stipulations herein, the other party has the right to terminate this agreement.

1. Is the fixing of prices of transactions subject to Party A's decision? And Why?

   _____.

2. As for the exclusive agency rights, what are the requirements stipulated in this contract?

   _____.

3. What are the materials that Party B shall, for the purpose of reference, forward to Party A regularly?

   _____.

4. If full payment is received, what requirements shall the paying of commissions satisfy?

   _____.

5. In which case could the agreement be closed?

   _____.

8 Translate the following sentences into Chinese.

1. Should such negotiations fail, such dispute may be referred to the People's Court having jurisdiction on such dispute for settlement in the absence of any arbitration clause in the disputed contract or in default of agreement reached after such dispute occurs.

   _____

   _____

2. The participants in the Joint Venture shall commence discussion with regard to the extension of the period of existence of the Venture and in the event of their agreeing upon such extension, they shall record such agreement in a written document signed by all of them not later than two years prior to the expiry of the current period.

   _____

   _____

3. The formation of this contract, its validity, interpretation, execution and settlement of the disputes shall be governed by related laws of the People's Republic of China.

   _____

   _____

4. Should all or part of the contract be unable to be fulfilled owing to the fault of one party, the breaching party shall bear the responsibilities thus caused.

   _____

5. The Attachments to this Contract shall be deemed a part hereof and shall be effective as any other provision hereof.

---

9 **Find out the basic elements of a sales confirmation, and analyze its differences from a sales contract.**

Case : Sales Confirmation

SALES CONFIRMATION

Date.................

No....................

Signed at................

The undersigned Sellers and Buyers have agreed to close the following transactions according to the terms and conditions stipulated below:

Quality No. , Name of Commodity and Specifications	Quantity	Unit Price	Amount	Time of Shipment
Total Amount				
Both Amount and Quantity% More or Less Allowed				

(1) Loading Port and Destination:

(2) Terms of Payment:

By 100% value confirmed irrevocable letter of credit available by draft at sight with transshipment and partial shipments allowed, to reach the Sellers _____ days before the month of shipment, with shipment validity arranged till the 15th day after the month of shipment, and to remain valid for negotiation in the loading port until the 10th day after the shipment validity. A _____% more or less should be allowed in the quantity and amount of the credit, and the word "ABOUT" should be mentioned before the quantity and amount. The terms and conditions in the L/C should be strictly in accordance with those in this contract.

(3) Insurance:

(4) Special Clause (s):

The Buyers   The Sellers

China National Textiles Import & Export

Corporation Shanghai Silk Branch

Please sign and return one copy of this Confirmation.

⑩ Extended Exercise

Fill in the following English contract with the information given in Chinese.

卖　　方：山东土畜产进出口公司
买　　方：鹿特丹食品进出口公司
商品名称：花生
规　　格：2008年产大路货 (FAQ: Fair Average Quality)
数　　量：50公吨
单　　价：成本+保险+运费鹿特丹人民币6550元
总　　值：
包　　装：双层麻袋装 (double gunny bags)
装 运 港：中国青岛
目 的 港：鹿特丹
唛　　头：由卖方选定
装 运 期：2008年11月
付款方式：不可撤销的即期信用证
保　　险：由卖方按发票金额的110%投保一切险和战争险
签订日期、地点：2008年4月12日于山东青岛
合同号码：CD1123

Contract No.:_____

Buyers: Rotterdam Foodstuffs Import and Export Company

Sellers: Shandong Native Produce and Animal By-products Import and Export Corporation

This contract is made by and between the Buyers and the Sellers, whereby the Buyers agree to buy and the Sellers agree to sell the under-mentioned goods according to the terms and conditions stipulated below:

Commodity:

Specifications:

Quantity:

Unit Price:

Total Value: RMB327,500 (Say RMB Three Hundred And Twenty-Seven Thousand Five Hundred Only)

Packing:

Time of Shipment:

Port of Shipment:

Port of Destination:

Shipping Marks:

Terms of Payment:

Insurance:

Done and Signed in _____ on this _____ day of _____.

6 Foreign Exchange

① Match the following trade terms with the Chinese equivalents.

1. FOREX	A. 场外交易
2. New York Stock Exchange	B. 汇率
3. Over-the-Counter	C. 杠杆率
4. EUR/YEN	D. 投机
5. Exchange Rate	E. 外汇
6. Speculating	F. 美元/日元
7. Leverage	G. 纽约证交所

② Choose the best answers.

1. The relationship between the exchange rate and the prices of tradable goods is known as the _____.

   A. purchasing-power-parity theory

   B. asset-markets theory

   C. monetary theory

   D. balance-of-payments theory

2. If the exchange rate between Euro and British pounds is 5 euro per pound, then the number of pounds that can be obtained for 200 euro equals _____.

   A. 20 pounds   B. 40 pounds

   C. 60 pounds   D. 80 pounds

3 Low real interest rates in the United States tend to _____.

   A. decrease the demand for dollars, causing the dollar to depreciate

   B. decrease the demand for dollars, causing the dollar to appreciate

   C. increase the demand for dollars, causing the dollar to depreciate

   D. increase the demand for dollars, causing the dollar to appreciate

4. Suppose Germany and France were the only two countries in the world. There exists an excess supply of French currency on the foreign exchange market. This suggests that _____

   A. the French balance of payments is in surplus

   B. the French balance of payments is in deficit

   C. the German balance of payments is in deficit

   D. there is an excess supply of German currency

5. Assume that the United States faces an 8 percent inflation rate while no (zero) inflation exists in Japan. According to the purchasing-power parity theory, the dollar would be expected to _____.

   A. appreciate by 8 percent against the yen

   B. depreciate by 8 percent against the yen

   C. remain at its existing exchange rate

   D. None of the above.

6. In the presence of purchasing-power parity, if one dollar exchanges for 2 British pounds and if a TV set costs $400 in the United States, then in Great Britain the VCR should cost _____.

   A. 200 pounds   B. 400 pounds

   C. 600 pounds   D. 800 pounds

7. The international exchange value of the U.S. dollar is determined by _____.

   A. the rate of inflation in the United States

   B. the number of dollars issued by the U.S. government

   C. the international demand for and supply of dollars

   D. the monetary value of gold held at Fort Knox, Kentucky

8. Given a system of floating exchange rates, rising income in the United States would trigger a(n) _____.

   A. increase in the demand for imports and an increase in the demand for foreign currency

   B. increase in the demand for imports and a decrease in the demand for foreign currency

   C. decrease in the demand for imports and an increase in the demand for foreign currency

   D. decrease in the demand for imports and a decrease in the demand for foreign currency

9. Which example of market expectations causes the dollar to appreciate against the yen; expectations that the U.S. economy will have _____.

   A. faster economic growth than in Japan

   B. higher future interest rates than in Japan

   C. more rapid money supply growth than in Japan

   D. higher inflation rates than in Japan

10. When the price of foreign currency (i.e., the exchange rate) is below the equilibrium level?

    A. An excess demand for that currency exists in the foreign exchange market.

    B. An excess supply of that currency exists in the foreign exchange market.

    C. The demand for foreign exchange shifts outward to the right.

    D. The demand for foreign exchange shifts backward to the left.

③ **Complete the following dialogues and practice them with your partner.**

A. 1 000 yen notes   B. the exchange memo   C. break

D. the exchange form   E. the exchange rate

Dialogue ①

A: Excuse me. Could you help me to _____1_____ this 100 U.S. dollar note?

B: Certainly. What kind of currency do you want?

A: Japanese yen. What is _____2_____ for U.S. dollar against Japanese yen today?

B: Our buying rate is 120 yen to one U.S. dollar.

A: How much would I get for this note?

B: 100 dollars make 12 000 yen. I'd like to know how I shall give it to you. Will twelve _____3_____ be all right?

A: Sorry. Would you mind giving me some big notes? I hope you will give me one 10 000 yen, and two 1 000 yen.

B: Certainly. Would you kindly sign _____4_____ giving your name and address?

A: Sure. Is it all right?

B: OK. Here is your cash and _____5_____. Have a check, please.

A: That's right. Thanks a lot.

B: You're welcome.

Dialogue ②

A. the currency appreciate hot money

B. fledgling foreign-exchange market

C. foreign-exchange market

D. currency forwards market

E. market supply and demand

A: You know, in China's _____6_____, the central bank sets a central dollar parity for the yuan each morning. For the past two years, it has allowed the currency to move barely a whisker from this rate.

B: But now it seems prepared to let it rise by up to 0.5% on any given day — not to let it rise by that much day after day.

A: Exactly, after Monday' statement, the PBOC let _____7_____ by over 0.4%, generating quite a bit of excitement.

B: At that rate the yuan would double in value.

A: Maybe next morning the central bank will set its parity to reflect the previous day's close.

B: But it decided that "_____8_____" needed a bit of a nudge. Heavy dollar-buying by the country's big state banks pushed the yuan down against the dollar, and this allowing the central bank to set a Wednesday morning parity of 6.81.

A: But on the other hand, the yuan may also slip on any day, as well as climb, against the dollar. Because the central bank is keen to deter "_____9_____" that might seep past the country's capital controls.

B: Some people think it has already succeeded. The _____10_____ expects the yuan to appreciate by only 2.2% over the next 12 months. It is a slender return given the hassle of getting money in and out of China.

4 **Read the following passages and decide which term each passage is describing.**

1. Direct Quotation (   )   2. Currency Speculation (   )
3. Purchase Power Parity (   )   4. Law of One Price (   )
5. Spot Exchange Rates (   )

A. Prices in countries vary for the same product but that they differ by the same proportional rate over time. The reasons suggested for this price difference include taxes, shipping costs and differences in product quality.

B. A foreign exchange rate quoted as the domestic currency per unit of the foreign currency. In other words, it involves quoting in fixed units of foreign currency against variable amounts of the domestic currency.

C. The rate at which a foreign exchange dealer coverts one currency into another currency within one or two business days.

D. The price of a given security, commodity or asset will have the same price when exchange rates are taken into consideration. It is another way of stating the concept of purchasing power parity.

E. Purchasing risky investments that present the possibility of large profits, but also pose a higher-than-average possibility of loss. A profitable strategy over the long term if undertaken by professionals who hedge their portfolios to control the amount of risk.

5 **Read the passage and fill in the blanks.**

One factor that obviously _____1_____ international business from domestic business is the use of more than one currency _____2_____ commercial transactions. If Marks and Spencer, one of the United Kingdom's leading department stores, purchase kitchen	1. A. distinguishes B. difference
	    C. notices D. detect
	2. A. on B. at
	    C. by D. in	

appliances ___3___ a British supplier, which is a ___4___ transaction that will be completed entirely in ___5___.

However, if Marks and Spencer chooses to purchase the appliances from Iowa-based Maytag Corporation, this international transaction will require some mechanism ___6___ exchanging pounds (Marks and Spencer's ___7___ currency), and U.S. dollars (Maytag's home ___8___).

The foreign-exchange market exists to ___9___ this conversion of currencies, ___10___ allowing firms to conduct trade more efficiently ___11___ national boundaries. The foreign-exchange markets also facilitate international investment and capital ___12___. Firms can shop ___13___ low-cost financing in capital markets ___14___ the world and then use foreign-exchange markets to convert the foreign ___15___ they obtain into whatever currency they require.

The foreign-exchange market ___16___ buyers and sellers of currencies issued by the world's countries. Anyone who owns money denominated in one currency and wants to ___17___ that money to a second currency participates in the foreign-exchange market.

The worldwide ___18___ of foreign-exchange trading is estimated at $1.2 trillion per day. Foreign exchange is being traded somewhere ___19___ the world every minute of the day. The largest foreign-exchange market is in London, followed by New York, Tokyo, and Singapore. These four location ___20___ for 65 percent of global foreign-exchange trading. It is supported that approximately 90 percent of the transactions involve the U.S. dollar, a dominances stemming from the dollar's role in the Bretton Wood System. Because the dollar is used to facilitate most currency exchange, it is known as the primary transaction currency for the foreign exchange market.

3. A. with   B. from
   C. toward   D. by
4. A. domestic   B. national
   C. state   D. country
5. A. Euros   B. dollars
   C. pounds   D. RMB
6. A. with   B. for
   C. in   D. from
7. A. own   B. using
   C. foreign   D. home
8. A. currency   B. cash
   C. money   D. dollar
9. A. content   B. direction
   C. facilitate   D. policy
10. A. thereby   B. cause
    C. as result   D. from
11. A. walk   B. pass
    C. across   D. move
12. A. flow   B. liquid
    C. wash   D. move
13. A. at   B. with
    C. from   D. for
14. A. around   B. by
    C. for   D. on
15. A. paper   B. strict
    C. funds   D. lagging
16. A. comprises   B. proves
    C. effects   D. durable
17. A. change   B. convert
    C. excel   D. differ
18. A. number   B. amount
    C. volume   D. groups
19. A. with   B. by
    C. on   D. in
20. A. imagine   B. foreseeable
    C. account   D. amount

6 Read the following passage and choose the best answers.

The Indian finance ministry's mid-year review, released this week, sees the external sector as a silver lining around the country's huge fiscal deficit. "Buoyant" and "encouraging" are the words used to describe three consecutive quarters of current-account surplus — the first in a quarter-century. Adding to that swelling foreign-exchange reserves and a stronger rupee, some are arguing that it is time for drastic liberalization of India's foreign-exchange system. They could be disappointed.

For most of the past decade, the nominal value of the rupee has been allowed to decline gently against the dollar, by about 5% a year, thus staying fairly steady in real terms. This year, however, it has been appreciating in real terms (and, since June, nominally as well). It would have done so more sharply had the central bank not been buying dollars with enthusiasm. Exporters of manufactured goods, obsessed with price competition from China, are aghast at the rise — and at the prospect held out by some forecasters that a sustained boom in India's IT exports means it will continue.

The rupee's recent strength is only partly related to India's prowess in software and the mushrooming of "business-process outsourcing" in such projects as call-centers. The chunky surplus on invisibles owes more to remittances: non-resident Indians, attracted by the stability of the rupee and its higher interest rates, have been moving their offshore deposits back home. Similarly, Indian companies are borrowing more in dollars without selling rupees forward to hedge repayments. The trade deficit, meanwhile, has been shrinking, as imports grow slowly.

The inflows have boosted foreign-exchange reserves by some $20 billion this year, to $66 billion, or 12 months' worth of imports. The size of this cover has started some calls for further liberalization of the complicate foreign-exchange controls that India still maintains, despite the move in 1993 towards rupee convertibility for trade purposes. In recent months, some controls have duly been eased. It is now simpler, for example, for individuals to open foreign-currency bank accounts, and for travelers to get hold of foreign exchange. And non-resident Indians have been allowed to take out money acquired through inheritance, or from rents and dividends.

Some commentators have taken all this as a indication of full capital-account convertibility. That is not on the cards. The experience of 1991, when India ran out of money, has left the central bank prefers to caution — an approach it felt was protected by the East Asian crisis of 1997-98. With war in Iraq looming and a chaotic oil market, some risk aversion is understandable. India's fiscal deficit — some 10% of GDP and widening — is another reason for moving slowly. Just as one rating agency, Moody's, is considering upgrading India's external debt, another, Fitch, has warned that its local-currency rating is under threat. Nor is it certain that opening the capital account would mean a weaker rupee. It might even attract more capital inflows. As India's exporters are learning, convertibility is a two-way street.

1. The expression "silver lining" (Line 2, Paragraph 1) most probably means _____.
   A. a side effect

     B. a favorable aspect

     C. a decorative line

     D. a comforting prospect

2. According to the text, the appreciation of the rupee in real terms _____.

     A. will lower its nominal value

     B. is bad news to exporters of manufactured goods

     C. means a sharper decline of its nominal value against the dollar

     D. will give impetus to the development of India's IT industry

3. The current account surplus owes to the following EXCEPT _____.

     A. the strength of the rupee

     B. the remittances of non-resident Indians

     C. the hedging activity of Indian companies

     D. the growing imports

4. Which of the following is TRUE according to the text?

     A. India's foreign exchange reserves increased more than three times this year.

     B. Individuals are now allowed to trade foreign currency freely.

     C. India now can tackle adverse events in the foreign exchange market better.

     D. India's foreign exchange controls are seen as a hamper to its economic development.

5. Which of the following is NOT a reason for India's slow response to calls for liberalization of its foreign exchange?

     A. Its increasing foreign reserve.

     B. Its past experience.

     C. Uncertainty of the oil market.

     D. Its growing fiscal deficit.

 Read the following passage and choose the best answers.

     Greece, economically, is in the black. With very little to export other than such farm products as tobacco, cotton and fruit, the country earns enough from "invisible earnings" to pay for its needed, growing imports. From the sending out of things the Greeks, earn only $285 million; from tourism, shipping and the remittances of Greeks abroad, the country takes in an additional $375 million and this washes out the almost $400 million by which imports exceed exports.

     It has a balanced budget. Although more than one Drachma out of four goes for defense, the government ended a recent year with a slight surplus — $66 million. Greece has a decent reserve of almost a third of a billion dollars in gold and foreign exchange. It has a government not dependent on united incompatible parties to obtain parliamentary majorities.

     But such happy highlights can't minimize the vast extent of Greece's problems. It is the poorest country by a wide margin in Free Europe, and poverty is widespread. At best an annual income of $60 to $70 is the lot of many a peasant, and substantial unemployment plagues the countryside, cities, and towns of Greece. There are few natural resources on which to build any substantial industrial base. There was warning some years ago that Greek statesmanship will have to create an atmosphere in which home and foreign savings will willingly seek investment opportunities in the backward economy of Greece. So far, most American and other foreign attempt have bogged down in the Greek government's red tape and shrewdness about small points.

Great strides have been made. As far back as 1956, expanding tourism seemed a logical way to bring needed foreign currencies and additional jobs to Greece. At that time I talked with the Hilton Hotel people, who had been examining hotel possibilities, and to the Greek government division responsible for this area of the economy. They were hopelessly deadlocked in almost total differences of opinion and outlook.

Today most of the incredibly varied, beautiful, historical sights of Greece have new, if in many cases modest, tourist facilities. Tourism itself has jumped from approximately $31 million to over $90 million. There is both a magnificent new Hilton Hotel in Athens and a completely modernized, greatly expanded Grande Bretagne, as well as other first-rate new hotels. And the advent of jets has made Athens as accessible as Paris or Rome — without the sky-high prices of traffic-choked streets of either.

1. The best title of this passage is probably _____.
   A. Greek Income and Expenditures
   B. The Improving Economic Situation in Greece
   C. The Value of Tourism
   D. Military Expenditures
2. Many peasants earn less than _____.
   A. $60 a week
   B. $2 a week
   C. $1 a day
   D. $10 a month
3. The Greek government spends _____.
   A. more than 25%of its budget on military terms
   B. more than it collects
   C. a third of a billion dollars in gold
   D. less than 25% of its budget on military terms
4. According to the passage, Greece has _____.
   A. a dictatorship
   B. a monarchy
   C. a single majority party
   D. too much red tape
5. Greece imports annually goods and materials _____.
   A. totaling almost $700 million
   B. that balance exports
   C. that are paid by tourists
   D. costing $66 million

Translate the following sentences into Chinese.

1. China's foreign exchange reserves rose by $154 billion during the first quarter, a record even by the country's own impressive standards.

   _____

   _____

2. Yet there are some clues that this may underestimate the building up of foreign assets, in turn suggesting "hot money" flows into China have accelerated and that holding down the exchange rate is getting harder.

   _____

   _____

3. At that time the currency of all member countries was based on a pegged rate with the U.S. dollar.

   _____

   _____

4. Due to exchange rate fluctuations of the early 1970's, the Financial Accounting Standards Board (FASB) was forced to study the issue.

   _____

   _____

5. If the external fund recommended by an attractor is convertible foreign exchange, the reward shall be calculated and paid on the basis of converting the foreign exchange into RMB according to the exchange rate on the foreign exchange settlement voucher.

   _____

   _____

 Read and answer the questions raised for the case.

Case & Question:

If Mr. A, the salesman of ABC Import & Export Company, has to carry $150 thousand out to Japan to pick up the goods there, could he carry the amount in cash?

If you are an employee in the international department of Bank of China, what suggestion would you give to Mr. A?

Expressions that may be used:

Foreign Exchange Control; Foreign Money Exchange; Customs Declaration

Write an article of at least 120 words on the topic of RMB Exchange Rates.

1. 人民币升值对中国出口的影响
2. 推动人民币升值的因素
3. 对此的看法

7 Management in International Business

1 Match the following abbreviated terms with the Chinese equivalents.

1. PDM	A. 知识管理
2. OPT	B. 风险分析
3. QM	C. 现金流量预测
4. KM	D. 产品资料管理
5. MRP	E. 物料需求规划
6. CFF	F. 质量管理
7. RA	G. 最佳生产技术

2 Choose the best answers.

1. In order to comply with the customer's specifications, the factory has to make several _____ in production.
   A. corrections   B. mistakes
   C. adjustments   D. defects

2. Competition in production among different firms can _____ the enterprises to improve the quality and increase the variety of their products.
   A. promote   B. stop
   C. prompt   D. make

3. When the organization sends its employees to some other countries, it _____ the responsibilities besides the basic functions of human resource management.
   A. takes with   B. takes on
   C. takes over   D. takes in

4. Competition _____ to the technical transformation and restructuring of the industrial production.
   A. contributes   B. causes
   C. helps   D. promotes

5. Under these conditions, the exporter has to make additional investment to raise the capacity of the _____ for producing export goods.
   A. buyer
   B. importer
   C. dealer
   D. manufacturer

6. Managers charged with building teams in different cultures need to assess the nature of the task _____ and, as much as possible, match the composition of the team to the type of task.
   A. performing
   B. to be performed
   C. perform
   D. performed

7. _____ is generally a team of individuals at the highest level of organizational management who have the day-to-day responsibilities of managing a company or corporation and hold specific executive powers conferred onto them with and by authority of the board of directors and/or the shareholders.
   A. Senior management
   B. Root-level Management
   C. Supervisory Committee
   D. Board of Directors

8. The dominant activity in the pre-selection phase of the employment cycle is _____.
   A. assessment
   B. performance management
   C. selection
   D. planning

9. We recommend you take a clean slate to identify all of the possibilities for your practice, _____ whether you have the money, time, people, or management to achieve them.
   A. with regard to
   B. without regard to
   C. with regard that
   D. without regard that

10. Effective business management requires that you continually _____ the issues that require attention, but it also requires that you _____ that not every action carries equal weight.
    A. address; recognize
    B. understand; reflect
    C. recognize; address
    D. reflect; understand

3 **Complete the following dialogues and practice them with your partner.**

Dialogue ①

A. management   B. training   C. identified   D. mention   E. assess

A: The middle managers I interviewed commented that they'd like training to cover more specialist areas. To be honest, though, I think they're involved in such a lot of training of new and existing junior stuff that they don't fully appreciate the benefits of receiving _____1_____ themselves.

B: Mm…could be challenging for us then.

A: Yes. Whilst welcoming the efforts of senior _____2_____, one of the marketing managers

I spoke to was quite open about his and his colleagues' views… he made the point that there was a widespread feeling that the motivation behind this new program wasn't clear… They thought it might be used as a way to _____3_____ their performance. Because of that, they hadn't been able to make up their minds either way about whether they were in favor.

B: OK. Well, let's think about the content of the program.

A: Right, well we must include sessions on the areas they've actually asked for. Let's have a look… customer care and presentation techniques were certainly on their list.

B: Didn't some of them _____4_____ negotiating skills as well?

A: OK. Let's kick off with what they _____5_____ as their priority areas — so we could do presentation techniques this time round and then put forward a proposal for sessions on negotiating skills and customer care and anything else they might want in the future.

B: That sounds good. We'll go with that.

Dialogue ②

> A. Feedback from our staff indicates some customers think our quality control is lax
>
> B. Send them a discount coupon for their next store purchase
>
> C. Has there been any follow-up on this issue
>
> D. dealing with the manufacturer right now
>
> E. hearing about too many customer complaints recently, even from some of our most loyal customers

Douglas: I called you in because I've been _____6_____. As a staff member, what do you know about this, Howard?

Howard: We've had a lot of problems with certain items from a new manufacturer. We've handled it according to the store policy of giving a refund or an exchange. _____7_____.

Douglas: From their point of view, they're right! It's not our fault, of course, but what are we doing about it? _____8_____.

Howard: We've contacted Purchasing, and they're _____9_____.

Douglas: That's not good enough! If we've had that many complaints, let's get the products taken off the shelves until the manufacturers clean up their act.

Howard: Alright. I'll talk to the department manager about it. Shouldn't be a problem, but it'll probably take them a day or two to restock the empty space.

Douglas: That's OK. Let's be pro-active with the customers who bought those products. _____10_____. And let's touch bases with our other recent customers to make sure that they're satisfied with our customer policies.

Howard: I'll get on it right away.

Douglas: OK. Thanks, Howard.

4 Read the following passages and decide which passage each sentence is describing.

1. Genuine feedback would release resources to be used elsewhere. (　)
2. Managers are expected to enable their staff to work effectively. (　)
3. Appraisals tend to focus on the nature of the face-to-face relationship between employees and their line managers. (　)
4. The idea that employees are responsible for what they do seems reasonable. (　)
5. Despite experts' assertion, management structures prevent genuine feedback. (　)

A. Performance appraisal is on the up and up. It used to represent the one time of year when getting on with the work was put on hold while enormous quantities of management hours were spent in the earnest ritual of rating and ranking performance. Now the practice is even more frequent. This of course makes it all the more important how appraisal is conducted. Human resources professionals claim that managers should strive for objectivity and thus for feedback rather than judgment. But the simple fact of the matter is that the nature of hierarchy distorts the concept of feedback because performance measures are conceived hierarchically. Unfortunately, all too many workers suffer from the injustices that this generates.

B. The notion behind performance appraisal — that workers should be held accountable for their performance — is plausible. However, the evidence suggests that the premise is wrong. Contrary to assumptions appraisal is not an effective means of performance improvement — it is judgment imposed rather than feedback, a judgment imposed by the hierarchy. Useful feedback, on the other hand, would be information that told both the manager and worker how well the work system functioned, and suggested ways to make it better.

C. Within the production system at the car manufacturer Toyota, there is nothing that is recognizable as performance appraisal. Every operation in the system has an associated measure. The measure has been worked out between the operators and their manager. In every case, the measure is related to the purpose of the work. That measure is the basis of feedback to the manager and worker alike. Toyota's basic idea is expressed in the axiom "bad news first". Both managers and workers are psychologically safe in the knowledge that it is the system — not the worker — that is the primary influence on performance. It is management's responsibility to ensure that the workers operate in a system that facilitates their performance.

D. In many companies, performance appraisal springs from misguided as assumptions. To judge achievement, managers use date about each worker's activity, not an evaluation of the process or system's achievement of purpose. The result is that performance appraisal involves managers' judgment overruling their staff's, ignoring the true influences on performance. Thus the appraisal experience becomes a question of pleasing the boss, particularly in meetings, which is psychologically unsafe and socially driven, determining who is "in" and who is "out".

E. When judgment is replaced by feedback in the true sense, organizations will have a lot more time to devote to their customers and their business. No time will be wasted in appraisal. This requires a fundamental shift in the way we think about the organization of performance appraisals, which almost certainly will not be forthcoming from the human resources profession.

5 **Read the passage and fill in the blanks.**

The principles of good management are applicable ___1___ financial-advisory firms of all stripes.

Strategy: the ___2___ for a business, which implicates all business decisions. Whatever the structure of the firm, the work of sales and marketing, financial management, operations, human resource, and information technology is always ___3___ achieved when the firm's strategy is completely apprehended. Management decisions get easier to make when you have a clear idea of ___4___ you want to achieve ___5___ a business. Financial management: managing the bottom line. Financial counselors incline to give short shrift ___6___ the financial management of their practices, perhaps because they simply ___7___ that all their difficulties will be solved with more clients. The dynamics of a ___8___ firm, however, require more dynamic management and a substantial understanding of what to monitor and act ___9___ to convert revenues into profits, cash ___10___, and transferable value. Human resource: achieving ___11___. In exploring human resource, we take into consideration the concepts of recruiting, retaining, and ___12___ staff at all levels. You can't be a true entrepreneur without leveraging ___13___ others. ___14___ leverage is a small portion of the difference between managing a business book

1. A. at   B. on
      C. in   D. to
2. A. significance   B. framework
      C. structure   D. component
3. A. better   B. well
      C. good   D. greatly
4. A. which   B. what
      C. that   D. how
5. A. like   B. with
      C. as   D. for
6. A. in   B. about
      C. on   D. to
7. A. conceive   B. expect
      C. propose   D. decide
8. A. benefit-oriented
      B. financial-advisory
      C. non-profitable
      D. value-adding
9. A. on   B. in
      C. at   D. to
10. A. amount   B. profit
       C. size   D. flow
11. A. accomplishment
       B. effectiveness
       C. insight
       D. excellence
12. A. punishing   B. registering
       C. cooperating   D. rewarding
13. A. on   B. off
       C. by   D. above
14. A. Which   B. This
       C. Hence   D. Such

and managing the business itself. Operations: managing risk, processes, and protocols. Managing operations effectively ____15____ on how well you combine together the tools and processes that have already been introduced by industry vendors, broker-dealers, custodians, and other counselors. Our review of the strategy, financial management, and human resource issues ____16____ your business will be conducive to your understanding of business operations, but this insight should be ____17____ with your own knowledge and the information that's been supplied by other experts in the field.

Information technology: processing information and communication. Both hardware and software have become ____18____ in helping advisers manage client relationships effectively and make more appropriate decisions on planning and implementation. ____19____ articles that allow you to apply technology more effectively to your practice have been written. The big challenge lies in how to frame your technology choices, how to apply new technology into your practice, and how to assess your ____20____ on this investment.

15. A. lies   B. focuses
     C. relies   D. regards
16. A. concerning   B. concerned
     C. given   D. proposing
17. A. linking   B. contacting
     C. integrated   D. combining
18. A. instrumental   B. conducive
     C. contributable   D. distributed
19. A. Few   B. A few
     C. A great deal of   D. Countless
20. A. back   B. return
     C. pain   D. benefit

 Read the following passage and choose the best answers.

It never rains but it pours. Just as bosses and boards have finally sorted out their worst accounting and compliance troubles, and improved their feeble corporation governance, a new problem threatens to earn them — especially in America — the sort of nasty headlines that inevitably lead to heads rolling in the executive suite: data insecurity. Left, until now, to odd, low-level IT staff to put right, and seen as a concern only of data-rich industries such as banking, telecoms and air travel, information protection is now high on the boss's agenda in businesses of every variety.

Several massive leakages of customer and employee data this year — from organizations as diverse as Time Warner, the American defense contractor Science Applications International Corp and even the University of California, Berkeley — have left managers hurriedly peering into their intricate IT systems and business processes in search of potential vulnerabilities.

"Data is becoming an asset which needs to be guarded as much as any other assets," says Haim Mendelson of Stanford University's business school. "The ability to guard customer data is the key to market value, which the board is responsible for on behalf of shareholders." Indeed, just as there is the concept of Generally Accepted Accounting Principles (GAAP), perhaps it is time for GASP, Generally Accepted Security Practices, suggested Eli Noam of New York's Columbia Business School. "Setting the proper investment level for security, redundancy, and recovery is a management issue, not a technical one," he says.

The mystery is that this should come as a surprise to any boss. Surely it should be obvious to the dimmest executive that trust, that most valuable of economic assets, is easily destroyed and hugely expensive to restore — and that few things are more likely to destroy trust than a company letting sensitive personal data get into the wrong hands.

The current state of affairs may have been encouraged — though not justified — by the lack of legal penalty (in America, but not Europe) for data leakage. Until California recently passed a law, American firms did not have to tell anyone, even the victim, when data went astray. That may change fast: lots of proposed data-security legislation is now doing the rounds in Washington, D.C. Meanwhile, the theft of information about some 40 million credit-card accounts in America, disclosed on June 17th, overshadowed a hugely important decision a day earlier by America's Federal Trade Commission (FTC) that puts corporate America on notice that regulators will act if firms fail to provide adequate data security.

1. The statement "It never rains but it pours" (Paragraph 1) is used to describe _____.
   A. the fierce business competition
   B. the feeble boss-board relations
   C. the threat from news reports
   D. the severity of data leakage

2. Some organizations check their systems to find out _____.
   A. whether there is any weak point
   B. what sort of data has been stolen
   C. who is responsible for the leakage
   D. how the potential spies can be located

3. In bringing up the concept of GASP the author is making the point that _____.
   A. shareholders' interests should be properly attended to
   B. information protection should be given due attention
   C. businesses should enhance their level of accounting security
   D. the market value of customer data should be emphasized

4. What puzzles the author is that some bosses fail to _____.
   A. see the link between trust and data protection

B. perceive the sensitivity of personal data

C. realize the high cost of data restoration

D. appreciate the economic value of trust

5. It can be inferred that _____.

A. data leakage is more severe in Europe

B. FTC's decision is essential to data security

C. California takes the lead in security legislation

D. legal penalty is a major solution to data leakage

 Read the following passage and answer the questions.

Commercial Operations Manager

This is an exciting opportunity for a Commercial Operations Manager based at our prestigious premises in the capital. You must bring your successful track record in contract management skills. Strong commercial awareness and communication skills are essential characteristics of your approach, as is the ability to motivate others. You will have considerable expertise with computers and your commitment to customer service will be strong. Relevant professional qualifications are a prerequisite for this post.

Recruitment Consultant

Recruitment consultancy represents a varied, stimulating and challenging career which will further develop interpersonal and commercial skills, allowing personal and professional growth. We offer unlimited career prospects within our management team here and overseas. Our individually tailored training scheme is one of the most advanced in the industry. We operate a reward system based on merit and profit-sharing, not commission or overtime. The remuneration package is designed to attract outstanding individuals to make a commitment to a long-term business relationship.

Production Manager

We are looking for a Production Manager to play an active role in our fast-growing company. We need a dynamic team player to help drive forward our firm commitment to continuous performance improvement and customer liaison. A background in engineering or processing would be highly advantageous. Working within a fast-changing environment, the ability to manage change effectively is a key requirement. The position is based on a rotating shift system and attracts a highly competitive salary and benefits package.

Services Manager

The person recruited to fulfill this new role in our fast expanding company will assume full responsibility for all the building and equipment at our head office. The company is currently considering relocation. You will be responsible for the management of communication systems including reception, co-ordination of secretarial support and management of all service suppliers. Some familiarity with computers is desirable. Personality, drive and the ability to set personal goals and high standards within a demanding working week are the main criteria. A degree and/or business qualification will be advantages.

Credit Manager

We are seeking a skilled credit professional with exceptional commercial acumen to play a vital role in our European program. You will deal with trade negotiations, account management and legal proceedings. Reporting directly to the Managing Director, you will develop and maintain our credit policy and take decisions on transactions within assigned authority levels for both existing and first-time client facilities and liaison. Based at our well-situated headquarters, with excellent IT support, you will be prepared to work hard in return for a rewarding remuneration package.

1. If you are good at encouraging colleagues, what post can you apply for?

   _____.

2. Which job requires one's working hours to be varied?

   _____.

3. Who will be responsible to senior management?

   _____.

4. What are the responsibilities of Services Manager?

   _____.

5. What post/posts requires/require knowledge of the computer?

   _____.

8 Translate the following sentences into Chinese.

1. Managing people well can bring companies better results and higher productivity, but this can be difficult to do.

   _____

   _____

2. Supply chain management (SCM) system is an important content of the current international enterprise management, and is also a development direction of national enterprise management.

   _____

   _____

3. To be precise, the terms "decision support systems," "executive information systems," and "OLAP (On-Line Analysis Processing)" are not quite synonymous — each has a slant that makes it a little unique.

   _____

   _____

4. It was a great way to learn a little about a lot of different subjects within the International Credit & Risk Management arena.

_____

_____

5. If a foreign auditor registered in other countries is necessary to be employed to undertake annual financial checking and examination, Party A shall give its consent. All the expenses thereof shall be borne by Party B.

_____

_____

 Read and answer the questions raised for the case.

Case: In the 1980s General Motors was suffering from high productive costs, deterioration in the quality, and a loss of market share. In 1984, GM entered into a joint venture with Toyota to establish a new company called MUMMI. GM then developed its newest U.S automotive division, Saturn. Later, the lessons learned from MUMMI were adopted by GM's German subsidiary, Adam Opel AG, when it built its new factory in the East German town of Eisenach in the early 1990s. The Eisenach operation is now Europe's most efficient auto assembly plant. And GM is now incorporating those lessons into three new factories in Argentina, China, and Poland, as well as its existing factories in Europe and the Americas.

Question: How does GM tackle the challenges of international strategic management?

 Extended Exercise

Write a short essay of about 200 words on the topic of "how to be a good manager" following the clues given below:

1. 爱岗敬业
2. 知识水平和管理能力
3. 勤劳善良

8 The Role of Culture in Business

1 Match the following terms with the Chinese equivalents.

1. acculturation	A. 个人主义
2. non-verbal communication	B. 文化适应
3. hierarchical structure of society	C. 社会阶层
4. high-context culture	D. 儒家
5. social strata	E. 社会等级结构
6. Confucianism	F. 高语境文化
7. individualism	G. 非语言交际

2 For the following ten statements, decide whether the communication is low-context (L) or high-context (H) according to Hall's high- and low-context theory.

_____ 1. People have a hard time saying no.

_____ 2. Paying attention to the status of the communicator is as important as the message itself.

_____ 3. The message is more important than the status of who communicated it.

_____ 4. Business is conducted only after enough time is taken for talking about family, health, important politics, etc.

_____ 5. People get down to business right away and often omit any "small" talk.

_____ 6. It is alright to say "I disagree" to your professor in class.

_____ 7. Use of intermediaries is common.

_____ 8. "I don't understand" is often used to voice disagreement.

_____ 9. If you want something, it's best to come out and ask for it.

_____ 10. Hinting at something is an effective way of getting what you want.

③ Complete the following dialogues and practice them with your partner.

Dialogue ①

> A. relationship B. acknowledge C. work ethics D. individuals E. cultural differences

A: Hi, Mr. Brown. You have been working in Korea for six years. Could you tell me how you feel about the differences in business communication styles and _____1_____ between Korean businessmen and American businessmen?

B: With pleasure. I think the work style of Koreans is relationship-oriented. Korean culture tends to emphasize the _____2_____ and to say "we'll push the details off until we have to solve them." The Western culture tends to look at the details upfront and try to say "If A, then B, if C, then D, if E, then F."

A: As to the leadership style of Korean and American managers, are there any differences between the Koreans and Americans?

B: I would say, Americans tend to focus on the _____3_____, with each person being responsible only for their own actions. In contrast, Koreans view work performance as a contribution to the group.

A: I think the American way of business usually appears to be more aggressive. Are you aware of these _____4_____ in your collaboration with your Korea colleagues?

B: Well, Koreans will often reply with a positive answer and show reluctance to give direct refusals, while we are more direct and straightforward than Korean people.

A: It is important for us to _____5_____ and respect these cultural differences in order to avoid cultural misunderstandings.

B: Yes, I believe understanding these cultural differences would better prepare American businesses for approaching the Korean market for the first time.

Dialogue ②

> A. And I believe they have learnt lessons from their Japanese experience
> B. Why it earns success in China and Korea but not in Japan
> C. In Japan, there are 90 shops per 100 000 inhabitants, compared to only 55 in the United States
> D. In Western business practices, growth is driven mainly by mass marketing the merchandise and using the high volume purchasing savings
> E. What about Japanese shopping habits

A: Carrefour is the second largest retailer in the world, but it didn't do too well in Japan. _____6_____?

B: I think its failure is rooted in its misunderstanding of Japanese business culture.

A: What do you mean?

B: _____7_____. However, in the Japanese market, consumers are very demanding and love new things. Sales trends can change practically overnight, and the regional differences are great. What Carrefour offered didn't appeal to Japanese consumers.

A: _____8_____?

B: Most of Japanese women don't work, so they can go shopping everyday. If they buy food once a week, they will feel bored. There are also a lot of small local shops, many of them open 24 hours a day. _____9_____.

A: So they should have done more research into the Japanese business culture. _____10_____.

④ **Read the following passages and decide which term each passage is describing.**

1. Culture shock (   )
2. Acculturation (   )
3. Cultural awareness (   )
4. Social stratification (   )
5. Corporate culture (   )

A. It is associated with the particular culture of an organization and is applicable to those who are employed in it. In other words, it can be defined as the culture of one group of people who share the same goal. This group of people could be a company or an organization. It plays an important role in determining employees' work behavior and the company's financial performance.

B. It is used to describe both the process of contacts between different cultures and the assimilation by one group of the culture of another which modifies the existing culture and so changes group identity.

C. This term expresses a lack of direction and uncertainty over what to do or how to do things in a new environment — about what is appropriate or not. We can describe this feeling as the physical and emotional discomfort one suffers when coming to live in another country or a place different from the original place.

D. It is the foundation of communication and it involves the ability of standing back from ourselves and becoming aware of our cultural values, beliefs and perceptions. It becomes central when we have to interact with people from other cultures.

E. This term refers to the hierarchical arrangement and establishment of social categories that may evolve into social groups and statuses and their corresponding roles.

⑤ Read the passage and fill in the blanks.

As with communication, culture is ongoing and subject ____1____ fluctuation; cultures seldom remain constant. As ideas and products ____2____ within a culture, they can produce change through the mechanisms of invention and diffusion.

____3____ is usually defined as the discovery of new practices, tools, or concepts that most members of the culture ____4____ accept. In North America, the civil rights movement and the invention of television are two good examples of how ideas and products ____5____ a culture.

Change also occurs through diffusion, or borrowing from another culture. The assimilation of ____6____ is borrowed accelerates ____7____ cultures come into direct contact with each other. For example, as ____8____ and North America share more commerce, we see Americans assimilating Japanese business management ____9____ and the Japanese incorporating American marketing tactics.

Although cultures do change, most change ____10____ only the surface structure of the culture. The deep structure resists major alterations. While ____11____ changes in dress, food, transportation, housing, and the like are simply attached ____12____ the existing cultural value system. Elements associated with the ____13____ structure of a culture — such as values, ethics and morals, work and leisure, definitions of freedom, the importance of the ____14____, religious practices, the pace of life, and attitudes toward gender and age are so very deep in the structure of a culture that they tend to

1. A. at B. to
   C. in D. from
2. A. resolve B. involve
   C. evolve D. evoke
3. A. Diffusion B. Creation
   C. Fiction D. Invention
4. A. eventually B. firstly
   C. quickly D. reluctantly
5. A. recreated B. reshaped
   C. reconstructed D. reinvented
6. A. which B. what
   C. that D. it
7. A. as B. with
   C. for D. since
8. A. China B. Canada
   C. Japan D. Mexico
9. A. habits B. exercises
   C. practices D. drills
10. A. effects B. afflicts
    C. jeopardizes D. affects
11. A. imperceptible B. visible
    C. subtle D. unseen
12. A. at B. in
    C. to D. with
13. A. deep B. shallow
    C. superficial D. medium
14. A. former B. past
    C. last D. previous

____15____ generation after generation. Even the demands for more liberal governments in China and Russia have their ____16____ in the histories of those countries. In the United States, studies ____17____ on American values show that most of the central values of the 1990s are similar to the values of the past 200 years. When ____18____ cultural change we cannot let ourselves be fooled just because downtown Tokyo looks much like Paris, London, or New York. Most of what is important in a culture is ____19____ the surface. It is like the moon we observe the front, which appears flat and one-dimensional, ____20____ there is another side and dimensions that we cannot see.

15. A. resist   B. assist
      C. consist   D. persist
16. A. stems   B. fruits
      C. roots   D. seeds
17. A. introduced   B. conducted
      C. concluded   D. examined
18. A. to analyze   B. analyzed
      C. being analyzed   D. analyzing
19. A. above   B. in
      C. below   D. at
20. A. and   B. or
      C. but   D. as

6 Read the following passage and choose the best answers.

CEOs of America Tricon Global Restaurants, the group that owns KFC and Pizza Hut, promotes Sichuan Beef Wrap at a KFC restaurant in Shanghai.

At present, there are more than 1 000 KFC restaurants in China, and they are increasing at an annual rate of 200. A new KFC restaurant opens every other day. Western counterpart McDonald's also continues to expand its premises.

Having arrived on the mainland in the early 1990s, McDonald's has more than 600 restaurants in nearly 100 cities. Although there have been fewer golden arches in America, its native country, in the past two years, China's McDonald's have grown at a rate of 100 restaurants per year.

The total income of fast food restaurants in China now stands at 180 billion RMB, and KFC and McDonald's account for eight percent. What kind of magic has brought them such success in China? How do they sustain growth rates? Their standardized business operation apart, the key is excellent inter-cultural management. KFC and McDonald's have absorbed the Chinese cultural elements of showing respect, recognition, understanding, assimilation and amalgamation, while maintaining the substance of the Western culture of efficiency, freedom, democracy, equality and humanity. This inter-cultural management mode, with American business culture at the core, supplemented by Chinese traditional culture, provides reference for international enterprises which need to adjust, enrich and reconstruct their corporate culture to enhance local market flexibility.

There are, however, certain conditions essential to inter-cultural management mode. On the objective side, there must be similarities in environment in order for the two cultures to connect and synchronize. KFC and McDonald's embody an accommodation of the fast tempo of modern life: a product of development and a market economy. Their resultant speed and efficiency are only meaningful in countries with a market economy. China's rapid economic development offered the environmental conditions corresponding to fast food culture. Services offered by fast food chains express their full respect for freedom, an American value, as well as the psychological statement of Chinese open-mindedness that yearns to understand and experience the Western lifestyle. The two cultures proactively crashed, connected, and assimilated. KFC and McDonald's use the localization strategy to re-express American business culture, with profound traditional Chinese cultural marks, catering to local customs on the basis of standardized management.

1. Which of the following statements is TRUE according to the passage?
   A. McDonald's promotes Traditional Beijing Chicken Roll at a KFC restaurant in Shanghai.
   B. KFC restaurants are increasing at an annual rate of 200 in China.
   C. McDonald's has more than 1 000 restaurants in China.
   D. On the average, a new McDonald's restaurant opens every other day.
2. The key to KFC and McDonald's enormous success in China is _____.
   A. standardized business operation
   B. the absorption of Western culture of efficiency, freedom, democracy, equality and humanity
   C. the absorption of Chinese cultural elements of showing respect, recognition, understanding, assimilation and amalgamation
   D. the excellent inter-cultural management
3. The inter-cultural management mode _____.
   A. uses Chinese traditional culture as the core element
   B. is supplemented by American business culture
   C. requires certain essential conditions
   D. needs to adjust, enrich and reconstruct corporate culture
4. The objective condition for implementing inter-cultural management mode is that _____.
   A. KFC and McDonald's embody an accommodation of the fast tempo of modern life
   B. fast tempo of modern life is a product of development and a market economy
   C. there must be similarities in environment in order for the two cultures to connect and synchronize
   D. speed and efficiency are only meaningful in countries with a market economy

5. The best title for this passage could be _____.
   A. The Rapid Development of KFC and McDonald's in China
   B. KFC and McDonald's Use of Localization Strategy
   C. The Influence of Western Culture on KFC and McDonald's
   D. KFC and McDonald's — a Model of Blended Cultures

 Read the following passage and answer the questions.

When you are hunting for a job, you want to look for and select a corporate environment that makes you comfortable, reflects your taste and style, and allows you to function and move along with ease. Whether or not you'll be happy working at a particular company will largely depend on how well you personally fit in with the company, and how comfortable you are with the company's corporate culture. Like a pair of new shoes, the company and you have to fit just right. Simply stated, there's no getting around it.

Every company has its own culture and your number one priority should be to understand it and blend into it. Quite simply, the corporate culture is the operating work environment that is set and shaped by the executives. It is interwoven with processes, technologies, and significant events. Some aspects of culture appear in visible ways but some are invisible. On one hand, visible culture are like the company dress code, work environment, work hours, ways for getting promoted, how the business world is viewed, what is valued and who is valued. This is the surface layer of culture. All of these can be seen and some are entrenched in the company's policies and regulations. Visible cultures play important roles in influencing its members' behavior and determining how its members interpret the environment. On the other hand, the far more powerful aspects of culture are invisible. It is composed of the beliefs, values, standards, worldviews, moods, internal conversations, and private conversations of the people that are part of the group. Invisible culture cannot be seen but it is more powerful than visible culture in influencing an organization's competitiveness and management efficiencies.

As a new member of the company, you cannot learn the visible culture by reading the organization's policies, but you can learn the culture by observing how existing members behave and inferring what behaviors are appropriate and inappropriate. For instance, if a majority of the existing members respect their seniors and obey their superiors without objection, you would also behave in the same way in order to fit into the organization culture and lessen their distinctiveness. If you want to be successful at a company, and enjoy where you work, you need to adapt to the company's culture.

1. What analogy is used to describe the process of your adapting to a new corporate culture?

   _____.

2. According to the passage, what does corporate culture refer to?

   _____.

3. What are the components the corporate culture at its surface layer?

    _____.

4. Why is invisible culture more powerful than visible culture?

    _____.

5. As a new member of the company, how can you learn its corporate culture?

    _____.

8 Translate the following sentences into Chinese.

1. In the West, clear delineation and classification of job responsibilities are instrumental in creating a strong company culture.

    _____

    _____

2. The increase in international business and in foreign investment has created a need for executives with knowledge of foreign languages and skills in cross-cultural communication.

    _____

    _____

3. When meeting someone in a Western business setting, conversation usually remains focused on business matters and business topics.

    _____

    _____

4. Clearly, perceptions and differences in values affect the outcomes of negotiations and the success of negotiators.

    _____

    _____

5. A corporation's culture determines and reflects the values, beliefs, and attitudes of its members, and these values and beliefs foster norms that influence employees' behavior.

    _____

    _____

Read and answer the questions raised for the case.

Case: Facing employees with diverse cultural backgrounds

Facts: Jonathan Brown has been chosen to set up a branch of his engineering consulting firm in Seoul, South Korea. Although the six engineering consultants that would eventually be transferred there were British, Jonathan is interested in hiring locals as support staff. He is offering a great salary with excellent working conditions. He gets some names put forward through contacts he has in Seoul. After meeting with them, he is surprised to find all of them turn down his offer. All preferred to stay with their current employers.

Questions: In your opinion, what are the reasons for this phenomenon?

 Extended Exercise

Please write a 150-word essay according to the following information.

Directions: Now we have more chances to communicate with foreigners.But how can we have a successful cross-cultural communication? Write a composition of about 150 words on the following topic: The Most Important Thing in Cross-cultural Communication

Unit 9 International Strategic Alliance

1 Match the following abbreviated terms with the Chinese equivalents.

1. NTB   A. 欧盟
2. NAFTA   B. 亚太经济合作组织
3. Mercosur Accord   C. 国内生产总值
4. EU   D. 非关税堡垒
5. GDP   E. 南方共同市场
6. APEC   F. 北美自由贸易协定

2 Choose the best answers.

1. People coming from Europe settled in ethnic _____.
   A. places   B. districts
   C. countries   D. locations
2. Which is the most integrated regional alliance in the world?
   A. APEC   B. NAFTA
   C. WTO   D. EU
3. Which country is NOT from NAFTA?
   A. Canada.   B. the United States.
   C. Guatemala.   D. Mexico.
4. NAFTA is a _____.
   A. free trade area   B. customs union
   C. common market   D. economic union
5. Which of the following can totally solve the problem of trade deflection?
   A. A free trade area.   B. A common market.
   C. A customs union.   D. A political union.

6. The highest decision-making body of the EU is _____.
   A. the Council of the European Union   B. the European Parliament
   C. the European Commission   D. the Court of Justice

7. China is not the member of the _____.
   A. WTO   B. APEC
   C. CAFTA   D. NATO

8. The interpretation and the application of the EU law and the treaties are ensured by

   _____.
   A. the Council of the European Union   B. the European Parliament
   C. the European Commission   D. the Court of Justice

9. APEC actually is a(n) _____.
   A. forum   B. conference
   C. alliance   D. region

10. The World Trade Organization (WTO) is an organization that intends to supervise and
    liberalize _____.
    A. international policies   B. international disputes
    C. international trade   D. international travel

 **Oral practice.**

Section A: Read the following cue cards and make a dialogue with your partner.

Cue Card Ⓐ

Situation: You are the manager of a large company. Your company is planning to launch a new extension to AU. You are going to call a meeting to discuss this project. Now you are assigning the tasks to your secretary.

Tasks:
- gather the full and detailed information of AU
- make a PPT to demonstrate AU
- investigate the prospects of new extension to AU
- make a report of the prospects

Cue Card Ⓑ

Situation: You are the secretary of the manager of a large company. Your company is planning to launch a new extension to AU. Your manager is going to call a meeting to discuss this project. Now you are assigned the task to make preparations for the meeting, and you have some questions about the assignment.

Questions:

- Whether the information needs to be printed or emailed?
- How many pages of the PPT need to be prepared?
- How detailed should the investigation be?
- When will the PPT and report be handed in?

Section B: Read and complete the following speech and practice it with your partner.

A. our security, including our economic security
B. I hope that at the APEC Leaders' summit this weekend
C. We are all in this together
D. We know that the successful launch of
E. Thank you for the invitation to participate

_____1_____ in this APEC CEO forum. It is good to see so many of you here. Indeed it was critical that the APEC Summit and this CEO forum proceed. Our presence here signals our determination not to be intimidated by terrorists, but rather to get on with the work of economic development and international cooperation in all its many forms, including trade.

_____2_____ we will make a strong commitment to collective action against terrorism. The terrorist attacks struck not against one nation, but against humanity, _____3_____.

_____4_____ is inter-linked. This year, in Shanghai, we must assert that trade and economic prosperity are also major forces for stability and confidence building.

_____5_____ a new WTO round will underpin confidence in the world economy and help stimulate growth.

This morning's session looked at the double edge of globalization, at striking a balance between efficiency and equity. Let me tell you how we in New Zealand are seeking to achieve that balance.

4 Read the following passages and decide which process each passage is describing.

1. Strategy Development ( )
2. Partner Assessment ( )
3. Contract Negotiation ( )
4. Alliance Operation ( )
5. Alliance Termination ( )

A. It involves determining whether all parties have realistic objectives, forming high caliber negotiating teams, defining each partner's contributions and rewards as well as protect any proprietary information, addressing termination clauses, penalties for poor performance, and highlighting the degree to which arbitration procedures are clearly stated and understood.

B. It involves winding down the alliance, for instance when its objectives have been met or cannot be met, or when a partner adjusts priorities or re-allocates resources elsewhere.

C. It involves studying the alliance's feasibility, objectives and rationale, focusing on the major issues and challenges and development of resource strategies for production, technology, and people. It requires aligning alliance objectives with the overall corporate strategy.

D. It involves addressing senior management's commitment, finding the caliber of resources devoted to the alliance, linking of budgets and resources with strategic priorities, measuring and rewarding alliance performance, and assessing the performance and results of the alliance.

E. It involves analyzing a potential partner's strengths and weaknesses, creating strategies for accommodating all partners' management styles, preparing appropriate partner selection criteria, understanding a partner's motives for joining the alliance and addressing resource capability gaps that may exist for a partner.

5 Read the passage and fill in the blanks.

Europe Day — a _____1_____, but also a chance to find out more about the EU and what it does, with events and activities _____2_____ all ages.

On 9 May 1950, Robert Schuman, French foreign minister, _____3_____ the press together for a major announcement. He called on France, Germany and other _____4_____ countries still recovering from the Second World War to pool their production of coal and steel. This was a major step _____5_____ the road towards lasting peace in Europe and the first _____6_____ towards later economic _____7_____. Today, this announcement — the Schuman declaration — is seen as the birth certificate of the European Union and, every year, 9 _____8_____ is celebrated as Europe Day.

For the 60th _____9_____ of the declaration, the EU institutions are in celebration mode, organizing concerts, dance shows, a giant quiz, information _____10_____ and all sorts of other

1. A. wonder   B. celebration
   C. ceremony   D. specialty
2. A. for   B. at
   C. in   D. on
3. A. cried   B. announced
   C. spoken   D. called
4. A. world   B. European
   C. Africa   D. global
5. A. in   B. at
   C. on   D. to
6. A. step   B. road
   C. side   D. trip
7. A. integration   B. development
   C. growth   D. promotion
8. A. April   B. October
   C. December   D. May
9. A. celebration   B. congratulation
   C. anniversary   D. ceremony
10. A. jumps   B. bulletin
    C. stands   D. announcement

activities.

In Brussels the ___11___ for festivities taking place in Belgium, various EU buildings will be opening their doors to the ___12___ on Saturday 8 May: the Berlaymont building (home to the European Commission), the debating chamber of the European Parliament and the ___13___ hall of the Council building where European leaders and ministers meet.

Younger visitors will be able to ___14___ a European-themed kite at the Parliament, or ___15___ biodiversity at the Economic and Social Committee. At the Commission there will be games to get them thinking about animal ___16___.

European culture will be in the spotlight at a conference organized by the Committee of the Regions — ___17___ of the many conferences taking place ___18___ the city. In the European Parliament, ___19___ will be hosting public debates. Meanwhile visitors to the Council can take part in a ___20___ of a meeting between national ministers: will they manage to draw up a European green-car initiative?

Film buffs will be treated to a feast of European cinema in all its richness at the seventh EuroCine festival, with 27 films from the 27 EU countries being screened in 5 European capitals.

11. A. base   B. foundation
    C. place   D. house
12. A. people   B. foreigner
    C. public   D. persons
13. A. major   B. important
    C. vital   D. main
14. A. do   B. make
    C. take   D. produce
15. A. explore   B. search
    C. investigate   D. look for
16. A. thinking   B. advantage
    C. facility   D. welfare
17. A. single   B. sole
    C. only   D. one
18. A. in   B. around
    C. at   D. up
19. A. attendants   B. participants
    C. members   D. anticipates
20. A. simulation   B. participation
    C. operation   D. anticipation

6 **Read the following passage and choose the best answers.**

Greenhouse gas emissions from EU countries have fallen slightly, the latest figures reveal. The core 15 member countries — members of the EU before 2004 — saw emissions fall overall by 0.8 per cent in 2006. Emissions are now 2.7 per cent down on the base year of 1990, according to the European Environmental Agency. But almost all of the 12 new members, most of them from Eastern Europe, saw their emissions rise, according to the latest available figures.

European Environment Commissioner Stavros Dimas said progress was being made and that the EU-15 were on course to meet the Kyoto target of keeping average emissions between 2008-2012 at least 8 per cent below 1990 levels.

Stavros Dimas said, "The recent emission decreases among the EU-15 are encouraging. Nevertheless, the emission increases in the majority of EU-12 countries are not helpful. The EU-12 have to bear in mind that they cannot rely on the successes of the past. Our targets for reducing greenhouse gas emissions after 2012 are for the EU-27 together and a continuous effort will be required by all members to achieve them."

The main reasons for the 35m ton fall in emissions were warmer weather, lower production of nitric acid and the introduction of new technologies.

Overall emissions from the 27 member countries fell 0.3 per cent, to stand 10.8 per cent below levels in the base year, which for some countries differs from 1990, and 7.7 per cent below levels in 1990 itself.

The drop, totaling 14m tons, was put down to a cut in nitric acid production, decreases in emissions from chemicals production in France and Hungary and lower overall domestic use of gas and liquid fuels.

But there was concern about a rise in emissions in EU-15 from the transport sector compared to a fall in the agriculture and waste sectors. Emissions from energy industries appear to have stabilized, while emissions from manufacturing industries show a slight decline.

The 0.8 per cent drop in EU-15 emissions between 2005 and 2006 at the same time as an increase in GDP of 2.8 per cent was achieved as further evidence that the EU has succeeded in decoupling emissions from economic growth.

1. The European Environmental Agency began to request the reduction of greenhouse gas emissions from _____.
   A. 2004   B. 2006
   C. 1990   D. 2008

2. What did Stavros Dimas' words mean in the third paragraph?
   A. The EU-12 should not release more greenhouse gases than the EU-15.
   B. The EU-15 are doing better than the EU-12 so the EU-12 are to blame.
   C. The EU-15 can release more greenhouse gases because of their successes in the past.
   D. The EU-27 should make a concerted effort to achieve their target.

3. Which of the following statements is NOT true?
   A. The emissions in EU-15 were rising in transport sector.
   B. The emissions in EU-15 were falling in the agriculture and waste sectors.
   C. The emissions in EU-15 were rising in energy industries.
   D. The emissions in EU-15 were declining slightly in manufacturing industries

4. The underlined word "decoupling" in the last sentence most likely means _____.

    A. connecting

    B. separating

    C. decreasing

    D. developing

5. What is the passage mainly talking about?

    A. EU greenhouse gas emissions fell slightly.

    B. The EU-12 should cooperate with the EU-15.

    C. Concerns about the greenhouse gas emissions from EU countries.

    D. Methods for reducing the greenhouse gas emissions.

7 **Read the following passage and answer the questions.**

The Arab League, officially called the League of Arab States, is a regional organization of Arab states in North and Northeast Africa, and Southwest Asia. It was formed in Cairo on March 22, 1945 with six members: Egypt, Iraq, Transjordan (renamed Jordan after 1946), Lebanon, Saudi Arabia, and Syria. Yemen joined as a member on May 5, 1945. The Arab League currently has 22 members and four observers. The main goal of the league is to "draw closer the relations between member States and co-ordinate collaboration between them, to safeguard their independence and sovereignty, and to consider in a general way the affairs and interests of the Arab countries."

The Arab League is rich in resources, with enormous oil, and natural gas resources in certain member states; it also has great fertile lands in southern Sudan, usually referred to as the food basket of the Arab World. The region's instability has not affected its tourism industry that is considered the fastest growing industry in the region, with Egypt, the UAE, Morocco, Tunisia, and Jordan leading the way. Another industry that is growing steadily in the Arab League is telecommunications. Within less than a decade, local companies such as Orascom, and Etisalat have managed to compete internationally.

Economic achievements initiated by the League amongst member states have been less impressive than those achieved by other smaller Arab organizations such as the Gulf Cooperation Council (GCC). However, several promising major economic projects are set to be completed soon. Among them is the Arab Gas Pipeline, scheduled to be accomplished in 2010. It will transport Egyptian and Iraqi gas to Jordan, Syria, Lebanon, and Turkey. The Greater Arab Free Trade Area (GAFTA),had come into effect on January 1, 2008, rendered 95% of all Arab products free of customs.

Economic development in the Arab League is very disparate. Significant difference in wealth and economic conditions exist between the rich oil states of the UAE, Qatar, Kuwait, and Algeria on the one hand, and poor countries like the Comoros, Mauritania, and Djibouti on the other. Arab economic funding is under development. As an example, the Arab League agreed to support the Sudanese region of Darfur with US$500 million, and Egyptian, and Libyan companies are planning to build several wells in this dry area.

1. What is the main goal of the Arab League?

   _____.

2. What is the food basket of the Arab World?

   _____.

3. What is the fastest growing industry in the region?

   _____.

4. Which organization initiated the most impressive economic achievement in the Arab world?

   _____.

5. Will you describe the economic development in the Arab League, please?

   _____.

8 Translate the following sentences into Chinese.

1. The value of world merchandise trade rose around 25% in the first six months of 2010 up strongly from the same period of 2009.

   _____

   _____

2. It has become the share understanding of East Asia countries to maintain regional peace and stability, develop the economy, science and technology, expand mutually beneficial cooperation, and promote common prosperity.

   _____

   _____

3. WTO Director-General Pascal Lamy said on 31 August 2010 that "current multilateral trade rules are still unbalanced in favor of developed countries".

   _____

   _____

4. The annual APEC summit photo session has seen some of the world's most powerful politicians dressed in a variety of costumes.

   _____

   _____

5. The highest decision-making organ of the African Union is the Assembly, made up of all the heads of state or government of member states of the AU.

   _____

   _____

Read and answer the questions raised for the case.

Case: Small businesses, center stage for European SME (Small Medium Enterprises) week

37 countries host events in support of small businesses and entrepreneurs.

Europeans looking to start a business or grow an existing company may want to check out some of the hundreds of fairs, conferences and workshops taking place during European SME week.

The week of activities is part of an EU effort to raise awareness of the types and sources of support available to small and mid-sized businesses.

The events include open days at some companies, providing entrepreneurs with a first-hand look at some of the challenges and rewards of running a business.

Some 99% of all European companies are small businesses, with fewer than 250 employees. As major employers and the main source of new jobs, they hold the key to getting the European economy back on a strong track.

Questions: Are SMEs so important to European Union economy? Will such an activity be held continually to promote small business and entrepreneurs?

 Extended Exercise

Search internet for the information, and make a report on China and APEC. You can write your report from the following aspects:

1. introduction of APEC
2. China's functions with APEC
3. prospects of APEC

10 Cross-cultural Communication

 Match the information in Column A with the choices in Column B.

Column Ⓐ
1. international communication
2. intercultural communication
3. cross-cultural communication
4. interpersonal communication
5. intra-cultural communication

Column Ⓑ
A. the comparison of cultural phenomena in different cultures
B. the communication between culturally similar individuals
C. interactions among people from different nations
D. face-to-face interactions among people of diverse cultures
E. the communication between two people

2 **Choose the best answers.**

1. People from _____ don't like to be touched when greeting each other.
   A. America   B. France
   C. Arab   D. Japan
2. _____ is not the key business value in the U.S.A.
   A. Collectivism   B. Individualism
   C. Low context   D. Egalitarianism
3. In business, "harmony", "face" and "relationship" are highly valued by Japanese. "Harmony" is not reflected in _____.
   A. individualism   B. teamwork
   C. preservation of good relationships D. group decisions

4. In German business culture, key values are not focusing on _____.
   A. facts
   B. tasks
   C. direct communication style
   D. relationship

5. To establish business relationship with Korea, _____ should be avoided.
   A. saving face
   B. harmony
   C. self-assertion
   D. relationship

6. In Russian business practices, _____ is considered inappropriate.
   A. co-operation
   B. praising someone in public
   C. equality
   D. mutual advantage

7. Stiffer upper lip is a term often used to describe the traditionally _____ portrayal of reserve and restraint when faced with difficult situations.
   A. Japanese
   B. French
   C. American
   D. British

8. _____ is not the characteristic of French culture.
   A. Tolerance of uncertainty
   B. Individualism
   C. Individuality
   D. Centralization

9. Australians generally avoid drawing too much attention to their _____.
   A. academic qualifications
   B. personal achievements
   C. business success
   D. All the above.

10. The key element in Saudi Arabian culture is _____.
    A. individualism
    B. collectivism
    C. egalitarianism
    D. respect and dignity

3 .Complete the following dialogues and practice them with your partner.

Dialogue 1

| A. urgent | B. delay | C. behalf | D. assistance | E. connect |

A: Madison Industries. This is Elizabeth Browning speaking. Can I help you?

B: Good afternoon. Could you _____1_____ this call with Mr. Williams, please?

A: May I know who's calling?

B: This is Mary Smile from ABC Computer Corporation. I'm calling on _____2_____ of Mr. Tom Winner, the general manager of our company.

A: I am sorry, Ms. Smile. Mr. Williams is now in a meeting. May I have your number and ask him to call back later?

B: I'm afraid Mr. Winner would like to speak to Mr. Williams right now. He has got an _____3_____ matter to discuss with Mr. Williams without _____4_____.

A: OK. Then, would you please hold the line?

(one minute later)

Ms. Smile, the line is through. Mr. Williams is ready to answer the call. Go ahead.

B: Thank you for your kind _____5_____, Ms. Browning.

A: You are welcome.

Dialogue ②

> A. getting ready for tomorrow's appointment
>
> B. I'm not big on formalities
>
> C. I've instructions not to mix pleasure with business on this trip
>
> D. he was unexpectedly tied up this morning
>
> E. I know how tiring they can be

A: Excuse me. Are you Mr. Thomas Johnson?

B: Yes, I am. From Northern Reflections of Canada, and you are Mr. Li?

A: No, sir, I'm not. I'm Liu Qing, Sales Manager at ABC Trading. Mr. Li asked me to come and meet you at the airport, because _____6_____. He is very sorry for not being able to come to meet you, and sends his warmest welcome to you.

B: I see. Well, it's very nice to meet you, Liu Qing. And please feel free to call me Thomas. _____7_____.

A: That would be my pleasure. Can I help you with your bags? We have got a car waiting outside.

B: Many thanks.

A: I hope you had a pleasant flight over, Thomas. I've traveled the trans-Pacific routes before, and _____8_____.

B: This one is uneventful, except for a little turbulence here and there. In fact, I feel as crisp as a new dollar bill.

A: Glad to hear that. Would you like an informal dinner with us tonight? Mr. Li asked me to inquire.

B: It's very nice of him, but truthfully I'd rather just spend a quiet evening in the hotel, _____9_____. I hope Mr. Li won't mind?

A: Not at all. He expected you'd need a little rest first. Just to confirm — you know that tomorrow's meeting is set for 9 a.m. , at our office? I will pick you up at the hotel at 8:15.

B: That will be fine. Liu Qing, thanks very much.

A: It's my pleasure. By the way, are there any sights you'd like to see while you're here? I'd be happy to show you around.

B: Well, _____10_____. But could we see the International Trade Center, and Zhongguancun Science & Technology Park?

A: That will be no problem. I'll make up arrangements for sometime later this week.

B: Thank you very much.

4 **Read the following passages and decide which variables in business negotiation each passage is describing.**

1. Negotiator Selection Criteria(   )   2. Complexity of Language (   )
3. Role of Individuals' Aspirations (   )   4. Decision-Making System (   )
5. Form of Satisfactory Agreement (   )

A. It can be "authoritative" or "consensual". In authoritative situation, an individual decides without consulting with his or her superiors. However, senior executives may overturn the decision. In consensus situation, negotiators do not have the authority to hammer down the deal.

B. In emphasis negotiators place on their individual goals and needs for recognition may also vary. In some cases, the position of a negotiator may reflect personal goals to a greater extent than corporate goals. In contrast, a negotiator may want to prove he or she is a hard bargainer and compromise the goals of the corporation.

C. There are two broad forms of agreement. One is the written contract that covers possible contingencies. The other is the broad oral agreement that combine the negotiating parties through the quality of their relationship.

D. These rules include negotiating experience, seniority, political affiliation, gender, ethnic ties, kinship, technical knowledge and personal attributes.

E. It refers to the degree of reliance of nonverbal cues to convey and to interpret intentions and information in dialogue. These cues include space, eye contact, gestures and silence.

5 **Read the passage and fill in the blanks.**

Result-cultures regard ends as more ___1___ than the means used to achieve those ends. The United States is where Management By Objective (MBO) had its origin, which isn't surprising ___2___ you consider the dominance of cause-and-effect thinking in U.S. culture. The basis of MBO is that you ___3___ your goals and then work out a strategy to achieve them. ___4___ the way you measure how close you have come. That's how you know you are making progress. Goals-oriented societies ___5___ a very high value on making progress, which ___6___ leads to methods by which to measure progress.	1. A. dazzling
	    C. normal
	 2. A. what
	    C. which
	 3. A. achieve
	    C. melt
	 4. A. In
	    C. After
	 5. A. place
	    C. produce
	 6. A. coincidently
	    C. quietly
		B. significant
		 D. minor
		 B. how
		 D. when
		 B. identify
		 D. fulfill
		 B. At
		 D. Along
		 B. result
		 D. debate
		 B. naturally
		 D. secretly

Measurement that seems logical to Americans may not seem so logical to others, however. The French often marvel at the American ___7___ for statistics and measurement of qualities they consider ___8___. The emphasis on measurement has led to an enormous ___9___ by business with figures of productivity and cost, which has led in turn to the high status and power accorded accountants. MBO has ___10___ from its former favor in recent years. Nevertheless, continuous measurement as a way to ___11___ quality has been successfully promoted by William Deming in the United States and much more successfully in Japan, ___12___ with less emphasis on measurement.

Not all cultures ___13___ the need to identify goals and work toward them. Management By Objectives hasn't exported very well. One reason is ___14___ the goals that matter to many people of other cultures include nurturing close relationship with co-workers. So ___15___ a proposed sale falls through, the relationship may have been strengthened by the contact made in the ___16___ to close it. In countries where power is concentrated at the top levels of organizations and is ___17___ according to personal favor, a healthy and strong relationship with the powerful one is ___18___ primary goal of every endeavor. This is particularly evident in formerly and presently communist countries. ___19___ good access to the party secretary, or a member in good standing of the party, was a conduit to ___20___ desired outcomes.

7. A. request   B. desire
   C. advantage   D. penchant
8. A. important   B. intangible
   C. humorous   D. ridiculous
9. A. preoccupation B. argument
   C. research   D. increase
10. A. decreased   B. fallen
    C. drawn   D. learnt
11. A. redeem   B. replace
    C. assure   D. examine
12. A. while   B. although
    C. which   D. actually
13. A. continue   B. meet
    C. feel   D. shrink
14. A. which   B. why
    C. that   D. whether
15. A. that   B. even if
    C. with   D. depressed
16. A. effort   B. field
    C. category   D. facet
17. A. discovered   B. measured
    C. identified   D. wielded
18. A. an   B. the
    C. a   D. /
19. A. Giving   B. Having
    C. Promoting   D. Turning
20. A. effect   B. effects
    C. to effect   D. effecting

6 Read the following passage and choose the best answers.

The tourist trade is booming. With all this coming and going, you'd expect greater understanding to develop between the nations of the world. Not a bit of it! Superb systems of communication by air, sea and land make it possible for us to visit each other's countries at a moderate cost. What was once the "grand tour", reserved for only the very rich, is now within everybody's grasp. The package tour and chartered flights are not to be sneered at. Modern travelers enjoy a level of comfort which the lords and ladies on grand tours in the old days couldn't have dreamed of. But what's the sense of this mass exchange of populations if the nations of the world remain basically ignorant of each other?

Many tourist organizations are directly responsible for this state of affairs. They deliberately set out to protect their clients from too much contact with the local population. The modern tourist leads a cosseted, sheltered life. He lives at international hotels, where he eats his international food and sips his international drink while he gazes at the natives from a distance. Conducted tours to places of interest are carefully censored. The tourist is allowed to see only what the organizers want him to see and no more. A strict schedule makes it impossible for the tourist to wander off on his own; and anyway, language is always a barrier, so he is only too happy to be protected in this way. At its very worst, this leads to a new and hideous kind of colonization. The summer quarters of the inhabitants of the cite universitaire: are temporarily reestablished on the island of Corfu. Blackpool is recreated at Torremolinos where the traveler goes not to eat paella, but fish and chips.

The sad thing about this situation is that it leads to the persistence of national stereotypes. We don't see the people of other nations as they really are, but as we have been brought up to believe they are. You can test this for yourself. Take five nationalities, say, French, German, English, American and Italian. Now in your mind, match them with these five adjectives: musical, amorous, cold, pedantic, and native. Far from providing us with any insight into the national characteristics of the peoples just mentioned, these adjectives actually act as barriers. So when you set out on your travels, the only characteristics you notice are those which confirm your preconceptions. You come away with the highly unoriginal and inaccurate impression that, say, "Anglo-Saxons are hypocrites" of that "Latin peoples shout a lot". You only have to make a few foreign friends to understand how absurd and harmful national stereotypes are. But how can you make foreign friends when the tourist trade does its best to prevent you?

Carried to an extreme, stereotypes can be positively dangerous. Wild generalizations stir up racial hatred and blind us to the basic fact — how trite it sounds! — that all people are human. We are all similar to each other and at the same time all unique.

1. The best title for this passage is _____.
   A. Role of Tourism in Understanding Between Nations
   B. Tourism Is Tiresome

    C. Conducted Tour Is Dull

    D. Functions of Tourism

2. What is the author's attitude toward tourism?

    A. Apprehensive.   B. Negative.

    C. Critical.   D. Appreciative.

3. What's the author's attitude toward national stereotypes?

    A. It will certainly help you understand the foreigners.

    B. They may actually act as a barriers.

    C. It will provide us with an insight into the national characteristics of the related peoples.

    D. It serves as a bridge between you and the unfamiliar foreigners.

4. The purpose of the passage is to point out that _____.

    A. conducted tour is disappointing

    B. the way of touring should be changed

    C. you notice, while traveling, characteristics which confirm preconception

    D. national stereotypes should be changed

5. What is "grand tour" thought of now?

    A. It works on moderate cost.

    B. It is treated as a local sightseeing.

    C. People enjoy the first-rate comforts.

    D. Everybody can afford to enjoy the "grand tour".

(7) Read the following passage and answer the questions.

    Biologically, there is only one quality which distinguishes us from animals: the ability to laugh. In a universe which appears to be utterly devoid of humor, we enjoy this supreme luxury. And it is a luxury, for unlike any other bodily process, laughter does not seem to serve a biologically useful purpose. In a divided world, laughter is a unifying force. Human beings oppose each other on a great many issues. Nations may disagree about systems of government and human relations may be plagued by ideological factions and political camps, but we all share the ability to laugh. And laughter, in turn, depends on that most complex and subtle of all human qualities: a sense of humor and certain comic stereotypes have a universal appeal. This can best be seen from the world-wide popularity of Charlie Chaplin's early films. The little man at odds with society never fails to amuse no matter which country we come from. As that great commentator on human affairs, Dr. Samuel Johnson, once remarked, "Men have been wise in very different modes; but they have always laughed in the same way."

    A sense of humor may take various forms and laughter may be anything from a refined tingle to an earth quaking roar, but the effect is always the same. Humor helps us to maintain a correct sense of values. It is the one quality which political fanatics appear to lack. If we can see the funny side, we never make the mistake of taking ourselves too seriously. We are always reminded that tragedy is not really far removed from comedy, so we never get a lop sided view of things.

This is one of the chief functions of satire and irony. Human pain and suffering are so grim; we hover so often on the brink of war; political realities are usually enough to plunge us into total despair. In such circumstances, cartoons and satirical accounts of somber political events redress the balance. They take the wind out of pompous and arrogant politicians who have lost their sense of proportion. They enable us to see that many of our most profound actions are merely comic or absurd. We laugh when a great satirist like Swift writes about war in *Gulliver's Travels*. The Lilliputians and their neighbors attack each other because they can't agree which end to break an egg. We laugh because we meant to laugh; but we are meant to weep too. It is too powerful a weapon to be allowed to flourish.

The sense of humor must be singled out as man's most important quality because it is associated with laughter. And laughter, in turn, is associated with happiness. Courage, determination, initiative — these are qualities we share with other forms of life. But the sense of humor is uniquely human. If happiness is one of the great goals of life, then it is the sense of humor that provides the key.

1. What is the most important of all human qualities?

    _____.

2. Why does the author mention Charlie Chaplin's early films?

    _____.

3. What is one of the chief functions of irony and satire?

    _____.

4. Why is laughter a unifying force in a divided world?

    _____.

5. What kind of life will you lead if you always keep a sense of humor?

    _____.

8 Translate the following sentences into Chinese.

1. One of the effective ways to solve such problems as human resource and cross-culture management is to increase the ability of studying and the quality of studying.

    _____

    _____

2. A totally new enterprise culture is the ultimate answer for resolving the problems of cross-culture team management.

    _____

    _____

3. The author of the book illuminated the important role a culture, especially, the common culture constituting part of the culture plays in helping students comprehend lexical connotation and the basic approach to the cultural acquisition, which promotes the cultivation of their cross-culture awareness.

   _____

   _____

4. We inquire into the far-reaching influence of cultural factors on personality and combine cross-cultural study with the discussion about the differences between culture and nation.

   _____

   _____

5. Generally speaking, company culture is a compass that guides us in our daily business decisions.

   _____

   _____

 Read and answer the questions raised for the case.

> **Case : Communication Problems**
>
> Mr. Tanaka was the first individual sent from his Japanese division to the U.S. The company designated his assignment as "developmental", and he viewed himself as a trainee. Soon after arriving at his new post, Mr. Tanaka was assigned to an internal trainer, an American who was responsible for Mr. Tanaka's learning according to a set of objectives jointly developed by the Japanese sending division and the American receiving division.
>
> Little time passed before Mr. Tanaka complained of adjustment difficulties and stress, and reported confusion and dissatisfaction over the content and purpose of his developmental problem. It became apparent that, even though there had been direct communication between the sending and receiving divisions regarding this program, there had been almost no mutual understanding. The Japanese sending division had put forward broad objectives such as upgrading Mr. Tanaka's ability to communicate in English and enabling him to improve his abilities as a global manager. These objectives were easy for the American receiving division to accept. But the American side interpreted the objectives quite differently from what the Japanese side had in mind.
>
> A closely related problem was that Mr. Tanaka's expectations regarding acceptable training methods were sharply at variance with the expectations of his American training.
>
> **Question:** Why is Mr. Tanaka confronted with adjustment difficulties and stress? What dose the case mainly indicate?

⑩ Extended Exercise

Have you ever thought about how to decline or refuse something in a business letters? The purpose in giving a refusal message is twofold: one, to convey the message; two, to retain the reader's goodwill. To accomplish these goals, you must communicate your message politely, clearly, and firmly. When you write a letter that conveys refusal, be sure to use a buffer in the first paragraph which does not suggest a negative message. In the second paragraph, present the case honestly and convincingly. The message is placed in a dependent place to deemphasize it. The letter ends with an action close, and make your closing original, friendly, and positive, avoiding any reference to the refusal case.

Try your hand now.

Suppose you are James Lee, and you are writing a letter to Mr. Thomas White who is Manager of Downtown Marketing Club. You have a long membership in the Club. You always play the role of a luncheon speaker there. But this year you can't take the part for the club because you have to interview marketing representatives and set up sales territories since your company is opening a branch in China. You will be comparatively free in June, July and August.

Answer Key

Unit 1   Trade Practice

1. 1. G 2. F 3. B 4. A 5. C 6. D 7. E

2. 1. C 2. D 3. A 4. C 5. C 6. C 7. D 8. B 9. D 10. C

3. 1. C 2. E 3. A 4. B 5. D 6. C 7. A 8. B 9. E 10. D

4. 1. B 2. D 3. E 4. C 5. A

5. 1. B 2. A 3. C 4. D 5. A 6. B 7. D 8. A 9. C 10. C
  11. B 12. D 13. B 14. D 15. C 16. A 17. C 18. B 19. D 20. C

6. 1. B 2. D 3. C 4. D 5. A

7. 1. National committees and groups form the global network makes ICC unique among business organizations.
   2. ICC members shape the organization's policies and alert their governments to international business concerns.
   3. Because the rules are developed by experts and practitioners brought together by ICC, and involve a long consultative process.
   4. They reflect the profound changes that have taken place in global trade since 2000.
   5. To introduce Incoterms 2010.

8. 1. 经证实的信用证或修改的电讯文件将被视为有效的信用证或修改，任何其邮寄的证实书将不予置理。
   2. 若电讯文件声明"详情后告"（或类似词语）或声明邮寄证实书将是有效的信用证或修改，则该电讯文件将被视为无效的信用证或修改。
   3. 单据的出单日期可以早于信用证开立日期，但不得迟于信用证规定的提示日期。
   4. 信用证中规定的各种单据必须至少提供一份正本。
   5. 提单的出具日期将被视为装运日期，除非提单包含注明装运日期的装船批注，在此情况下，装船批注中注明的日期将被视为装运日期。

9. Company B has the right to do so, because the loss in this case was the fault of Company A. Under the term of CFR, the seller takes the obligation to deliver the goods as per the transportation terms in sales contract, the buyer on the other end, should insure the goods as soon as the goods are loaded on the ship. The shipping notice is particularly important in the CFR contract, because under such contract, the delivery and the insurance are taken by the seller and the buyer respectively, and the time of delivery is very important to the insurance. Therefore, the seller should send the shipping advice to the buyer immediately after he effect the shipment, then the buyer can insure the goods in time. In this case, because the seller didn't send the shipping documents after he delivered goods, the goods damaged before the insurance arranged, the seller should take all responsibility to the loss.

10. 1. The form of L/C should not be "revocable", because the UCP 600 has defined that all the L/C should be irrevocable, which is different from UCP500.

2. The expiry date of the L/C is not in line with the latest date of delivery, because if they are the same day or too close, the seller may have not enough time to present the shipping documents to the bank for negotiation. Usually, the seller will ask the buyer to extend the expiry date.

Unit 2　Trade Policy

1. 1. H　2. F　3. D　4. G　5. A　6. B　7. C　8. E

2. 1. B　2. C　3. D　4. B　5. A　6. C　7. A　8. D　9. B　10. B

3. 1. D　2. A　3. B　4. E　5. C　6. E　7. D　8. B　9. C　10. A

4. 1. C　2. E　3. D　4. A　5. B

5. 1. A　2. B　3. B　4. D　5. C　6. C　7. A　8. B　9. C　10. A
　　11. C　12. B　13. D　14. A　15. B　16. A　17. C　18. D　19. A　20. B

6. 1. B　2. D　3. A　4. C　5. A

7. 1. The large scale processing trade policy contraction plan.
2. The processing trade holds a very higher percentage.
3. It has supplied people with a great number of job opportunities.
4. The new route for industrialization.
5. Because the foreign-invested enterprises are dominant in the processing industry.

8. 1. 其他许多涉及和中国进行贸易的方方面面的新法规已经颁布或生效，其目的是为了履行中国加入世贸组织的承诺。
2. 与此同时，省级和地方当局还在审议有关法律法规，看它们是否符合国家法律。
3. 美国对外援助的支持者们将它视为美国出口商创造新的市场，防止危机及推进民主和繁荣的工具。
4. 贸易壁垒仍然很高，尤其是在服务和农业部门，美国生产者尤其具有竞争力。
5. 统治者坚持认为贸易政策与劳工与环境标准之间不应该有联系。

9. The lesson from the post-war experience of South Korea is clear: The prolonged era of remarkable growth was associated with progressive liberalization, not enduring protection. After an initial phase of inward orientation, South Korea opened its economies to international competition. By doing so, South Korea achieved rates of economic growth rarely seen in world history. Protection was not eliminated overnight, and evidence suggests that residual protection detracted from stunning overall performance.

10.	According to the statistics of the table, from January to November in 2009, the total export-import volume of the textiles and garments amounts to 163.64 billion dollars, down by 11% than in the same period of last year. The export is 150.25 billion dollars and the Import is 13.39 billion, down by 11.4% and 10.7% respectively, gaining the surplus of $1368.6. From the trend, it is very difficult to turn the negative figure in the export to a positive one this year.

The slum in export indicates that the worldwide financial crisis has severely impacted our textiles and garments export businesses. The serious condition of the foreign trade shows that it is very important and urgent for us to start domestic demand and promote domestic consumption and investment. Though domestic demand has the broad prospects, it needs time and process to achieve its goals.

Unit 3   *Global Market Place*

1. 1. E　2. G　3. D　4. A　5. F　6. B　7. C

2. 1. A　2. A　3. D　4. D　5. C　6. B　7. A　8. B　9. C　10. B

3. 1. D　2. E　3. B　4. A　5. C　6. C　7. B　8. E　9. D　10. A

4. 1. B　2. A　3. D　4. E　5. C

5. 1. A　2. C　3. D　4. B　5. D　6. B　7. A　8. C　9. D　10. C
　　11. B　12. C　13. D　14. A　15. A　16. D　17. C　18. D　19. A　20. A

6. 1. D　2. C　3. B　4. A　5. D

7. 1. Greater efficiency and lower prices for consumers.

2. The lower production costs resulting from the greater production scale for an enlarged market.

3. Because a common market allows factors of production to flow freely across borders.

4. Economic gains and a higher degree of cross-cultural understanding.

5. Because it may reduce the opportunities for poorer countries and lead to the brain-drain phenomenon.

8. 1. 根据那些最早进入新兴市场公司的经验，投资者知道他们不得不面对以下各种潜在的困难：各种地方利益之间的冲突，超负荷运转的基础设施，技术人员的流失，复杂的供应链，陌生的本地人力资源实践和交流障碍。

2. 这些在开发规模经济中遇到的困难，缩短了在华跨国公司与具有强大地方优势和地方市场基础的中国企业间的距离。

3. 全球市场有一套它自己的经济规律 —— 经济开放，解除管制和经济私有化，以便使本国经济更加具有竞争力，吸引更多的外国投资。

4. 尽管整个东亚和拉丁美洲的前景令人乐观，但将占世界压倒优势的进口递增市场却可能减少到不足12个，我们把这些市场称作"大型新兴市场"。

5. 虽然作为市场也作为竞争对手，欧洲对美国极为重要，但我们也一定要认识到，其作为一支谋求开放全球市场和构成全球经济结构的力量，对我们也极为重要。

9. Russia, as an emerging market, is changing from a centrally planned economy to a market-oriented economy. Opening-up policies and the conversion of government monopolies into market-driven activities help attract foreign investment and spur economic development. The statistics cited in the case illustrate that Russia is witnessing a vast economic leap forward along the market-driven line. However, Russia still faces big challenges such as controlling corruption in the process of privatization, capital flight, and taking economic reforms. It still has a long way to go to become a market economy.

10.   China's Economic Development and the Stability of the Renminbi

As shown by the first graph, the exchange rate of the Yuan (RMB) rose dramatically form 5.2 against one dollar to around 8.4 during 1990 and 1995, and then has been falling slightly to 7.3 in 2010. Despite the Asian financial turmoil and its negative impact on China's economic development, China has given her pledge to maintain the stability of the Renminbi's exchange rate.

China's refusal to devalue the Yuan is a rational policy based on the country's domestic economic conditions. Owing to 30 years of reform and opening-up, China's GDP surged from 7 447.26 billion Yuan in 1999 to 4 222 000 billion in 2009. China's foreign exchange reserves today have hit more than US$1 950 billion. This enabled China to stand the trials of the Asian financial crisis, shielding the Renminbi from devaluation. China's effort to maintain the stability of the Yuan, in the long run, is beneficial not only to the country's economic development but also to that of the whole world.

Unit 4　Trade Procedure

1. 1. E　2. G　3. F　4. A　5. C　6. B　7. D

2. 1. D　2. C　3. D　4. D　5. B　6. D　7. B　8. A　9. B　10. D

3. 1. C　2. A　3. D　4. B　5. E　6. C　7. E　8. B　9. D　10. A

4. 1. E　2. C　3. D　4. A　5. B

5. 1. C　2. B　3. A　4. D　5. C　6. B　7. A　8. D　9. B　10. D

   11. B　12. C　13. C　14. D　15. A　16. C　17. B　18. C　19. D　20. D

6. 1. the principle of insurable interest; the principle of utmost good faith; the principle of indemnity

2. we know the sales terms which have been arranged

3. discovering at what point the property passes from one person to another

4. restore a person who suffered a loss into the same position as he was in before the loss occurred — not into a better position

5. a profit that could have been earned on the capital tied up in the transaction

7. 1. T   2. F   3. F   4. T   5. T

8. 1. 货物保险通常虽不使用投保申请单，但许多公司的确使用过渡性申请书列出它们所需的信息。

2. 信用证确保在受益人履行了信用证规定的条款与条件的情况下向其支付货款。

3. 尽管信用证在要求提交银行的单据中对发货的质量和数量已有规定，但这还是有赖于卖方的诚实守信，因为货物的制造、包装和装船都是有卖方负责的。

4. 出具收货人抬头提单是为了确保只有提单抬头上的收货人才能提取该提单项下的货物。

5. 若运输的为非商业出售的货物，如样品或展品之类，或是特别贵重的物品，就要使用收货人抬头提单。

9. In this case, the shipping company B should compensate Company C because it issued the clean B/L which is the final proof of the goods' condition. If Company B truly has the sound evidence that the short-weight is caused by Company A, it should compensate Company C first and then file a claim against Company A for compensation.

10. Dear Mr. Finch,

Our order No. 123 for 30 cartons of woolen carpets was received on Oct. 15. But we regret to say that 11 cartons were found broken and the carpets in them were soiled. This was obviously due to improper packing.

Needless to say, we have suffered a great loss from this as we cannot possibly sell the merchandise in this condition to our customers. We, therefore, have to ask you to give us a 15% discount on the invoice value or we will have to return the whole lot of goods to you and ask for replacement.

We hope you will give our request your most favorable consideration and let us have your decision at an early date.

Sincerely yours,

××××

Unit 5   *Business Contract*

1. 1. C   2. F   3. A   4. G   5. B   6. D   7. E

2. 1. D   2. B   3. C   4. A   5. C   6. B   7. B   8. A   9. D   10. D

3. 1. C   2. E   3. D   4. A   5. B   6. B   7. C   8. A   9. D   10. E

4. 1. C   2. B   3. D   4. E   5. A

5. 1. A   2. D   3. C   4. B   5. A   6. D   7. B   8. B   9. D   10. B
   11. A 12. D 13. B 14. C 15. C 16. B 17. C 18. B 19. A   20. C

6. 1. T   2. T   3. F   4. T   5. F

7. 1. No, the price shall be fixed through negotiations between Party B and the buyer, and Party A has the right to confirm it.

2. 1) Party A shall not sell or export the commodity to customers in China through channels other than Party B. 2) Party B shall not sell, distribute or promote the sales of any products similar to the commodity in and outside China. 3) Party A shall refer to Party B any enquiries for the commodity in question from other firms in China.

3. Party B shall forward the reports on market reports, samples of similar commodity offered by other suppliers, together with their copies, sales position and advertising materials.

4. Party A shall pay Party B a 5% commission on the net invoiced selling price.

5. If one of the two parties has violated the stipulated clauses, the agreement could be closed.

8. 1. 如果协商未果，合同中又无仲裁条款约定或争议发生后未就仲裁达成协议的，可将争议提交有管辖权的人民法院裁决。

2. 就本合资企业的存续时限的延期问题，各方应进行讨论；一旦各方就此达成一致，应形成书面协议，由各方在本合同期限到期之前的两年内签字生效。

3. 本合同的订立、效力、解释、履行和争议的解决均受中华人民共和国法律的管辖。

4. 由于一方的过失，造成本合同不能履行或不能完全履行时，由过失一方承担违约责任。

5. 本合同的附件应被视为本合同的一部分，与其他条款有同样效力。

9. This copy typically embodies the basic elements in a sales confirmation, which involves only the main clauses: the beginning (including date, number, etc.), the body (including basic information about the products such as name, specification, quality and quantity, unit price, etc, and also other main clauses such as terms of payment, insurance) and the ends (including the signature of both parties).

However, in terms of the sales contract, the formality is higher than the confirmation. It involves the beginning part (including the title, number, date, place, preamble, etc), the body (including the main clauses such as description of goods, quality, quantity, packing, price, shipment, insurance, payment, inspection, and other not necessarily involved common clauses such as claims and disputes, arbitration and force majeure, etc.) and finally the ending (including the languages adopted, validity, signatures and notices, etc.)

10. Contract No.: CD1123 _____

Buyers: Rotterdam Foodstuffs Import and Export Company,

Sellers: Shandong Native Produce and Animal By-products Import and Export Corporation

This contract is made by and between the Buyers and the Sellers, whereby the Buyers agree to buy and the Sellers agree to sell the under-mentioned goods according to the terms and conditions stipulated below:

Commodity: Groundnuts

Specifications: FAQ 2008 Crop

Quantity: 50 m/t

Unit Price: at RMB6 550 / mt CIF Rotterdam

Total Value: RMB327,500 (Say RMB Three Hundred And Twenty-Seven Thousand Five Hundred Only)

Packing: In double gunny bags

Time of Shipment: During November 2008

Port of Shipment: Qingdao of China

Port of Destination: Rotterdam

Shipping Marks: At seller's option

Terms of Payment: By irrevocable L / C available by draft at sight

Insurance: To be covered by the Sellers for 110% of the invoice value against All Risks and War Risk

Done and Signed in ___Qingdao___ on this ___12th___ day of ___April, 2008_____.

Unit 6   *Foreign Exchange*

1. 1. E   2. G   3. A   4. F   5. B   6. D   7. C

2. 1. A   2. B   3. A   4. B   5. B   6. D   7. C   8. A   9. B   10. A

3. 1. C   2. E   3. A   4. D   5. B   6. C   7. A   8. E   9. B   10. D

4. 1. B   2. E   3. A   4. D   5. C

5. 1. A   2. D   3. B   4. A   5. C   6. B   7. D   8. A   9. C   10. A

　　11. C   12. A   13. D   14. A   15. C   16. A   17. B   18. C   19. D   20. C

6. 1. D   2. B   3. D   4. C   5. A

7. 1. B   2. B   3. A   4. C   5. A

8. 1. 今年第一季度，中国外汇储备增长1540亿美元，即便按照中国自己的惊人标准，这也是一个创纪录的数字。

2. 然而，一些迹象表明，这可能低估了外汇资产的增长，进而说明"热钱"涌入中国的速度有所加快，而压低汇率的难度正不断加大。

3. 当时所有成员国的货币币值都是绑定在对美元的固定汇率上。

4. 20世纪70年代的汇率波动使得财务会计准则委员会对此展开研究。

5. 如引资者引进的外来资金为可兑换外币，则奖赏将按该笔外币结汇单的汇率折为人民币计付。

9. 　　First, A cannot take USD150 000 in cash out of China to Japan because of China's foreign exchange control policy which requires declaration for carrying large amounts of foreign currency to outside of China.

　　Second, A cannot pick up the cargoes valued at USD150 000 from Japan destined to China because it is an international business deal and it should be declared to China Customs.

　　So, A should sign a contract with the Japanese supplier who should ship the cargoes to China.

A will declare the shipment to China's customs, and then arrange international settlement through banks under foreign exchange policy.

10.   For quite a number of years, RMB's stable exchange rate has played a very good role, making China one of the biggest beneficiaries from international business. RMB's rapid increase in foreign exchange reserves plus capital controls helped China weather the Asian financial crisis. In particular, after joining the World Trade Organization, the fixed exchange rate also helped China rise as a trading power. So, if RMB's exchange rate rose rapidly in a short time, it would increase the cost of exports weakening the competitiveness of Chinese goods in the globe market.

However, for the better development of China's economy, a reasonable rise of RMB exchange rate is also necessary. The reasonable rate rising will help the upgrading of industries of China.

Generally, the upward revaluation of RMB will give Chinese economy more purchasing power, but it will also cause the imbalance as well. If this imbalance continues, the accumulated risk of Chinese economy as a whole will be growing. So we should be clear that there is active as well as negative side of the upward revaluation of RMB to China's economy. We will allow the RMB rate to rise, but it should be our decision on when it is the best time to do it and how much is reasonable for the rate rising.

Unit 7   Management in International Business

1. 1. D   2. G   3. F   4. A   5. E   6. C   7. B

2. 1. C   2. C   3. C   4. A   5. D   6. B   7. A   8. D   9. B   10. A

3. 1. B   2. A   3. E   4. D   5. C   6. E   7. A   8. C   9. D   10. B

4. 1. E   2. C   3. D   4. B   5. A

5. 1. D   2. B   3. A   4. B   5. C   6. D   7. A   8. B   9. A   10. D
    11. B 12. D 13. B 14. D 15. C 16. A 17. C 18. A 19. C 20. B

6. 1. D   2. A   3. B   4. A   5. D

7. 1. Commercial operations manager.
    2. Production manager.
    3. Credit manager.
    4. Services manager will be responsible for the management of communication systems including reception, co-ordination of secretarial support and management of all service suppliers.
    5. Commercial operations manager and services manager

8. 1. 管好人可以给公司带来更好的结果和更高的生产效率，但是这一点可能很难做到。
    2. 供应链管理系统（简称SCM）是当前国际企业管理的重要内容，也是国家企业管理的发展方向。
    3. 严格地说，"决策支持系统"、"主管信息系统"和"在线分析处理系统"这些术语并非完全相同，每个术语都有其侧重点，使得它们有自身的独特性。

4. 对国际信用风险管理领域的不同课程都学习了解一点，这绝对是一个非常好的途径。

5. 如果需要聘请在其他国家注册的审计师对年度财务进行审查，甲方应同意，其所需费用由乙方负担。

9. This case provides a dramatic example of how GM utilized worldwide learning to address the challenges of international strategic management facing GM in the 1980s. Worldwide learning required the transfer of information and experiences from the parent to each subsidiary and from each subsidiary to the parent. There were mainly two strategies that GM adopted: home replication and multi-domestic strategy. The home replicate strategy was predicated on the parent company's transferring the firm's core competencies to its foreign subsidiaries. The multi-domestic strategy decentralized power to the local subsidiaries so that they could respond easily to local conditions. GM got its experience from MUMMI - a joint venture with Toyota. Then it transferred its successful experience to its subsidiaries. In this way, it not only tackled the problems of high productive costs, deterioration in the quality of its vehicles, but also competed successfully with its rivals at domestic and foreign markets, and finally, it achieved global integration of its activities.

10.
How to Be A Good Manager

There are basically at least four attributes that a person should possess in order to become a good manager.

First, one should like the profession of management. Although it may be physically and emotionally draining, and filled with challenges and disappointments, it can be an exhilarating experience that allows one to make contributions to the development and success of an organization.

Second, good managers should possess substantial knowledge and solid organizational skills, which may be gained through a broad education or diverse experiences. It will help them make right decisions.

Third, hard-working is another attribute for good managers. Managers should have certain talents, for instance, the ability to communicate well, or to decipher complex mathematical computations. But unless they have the determination to maximize and market their talents, they may waste their talents.

Finally, a good manager should be a good person. The most important attribute that determines one's success or failure as a manager is the ability to be honest. He should embrace the purest and noblest intentions for the employees.

Only with those four attributes can employees feel a sense of trust in their managers and managers a sense of duty to their employees.

Unit 8   The Role of Culture in Business

1. 1. B   2. G   3. E   4. F   5. C   6. D   7. A

2. 1. H   2. H   3. L   4. H   5. L   6. L   7. H   8. H   9. L   10. H

3. 1. C   2. A   3. D   4. E   5. B   6. B   7. D   8. E   9. C   10. A

4. 1. C   2. B   3. D   4. E   5. A

5. 1. B   2. C   3. D   4. A   5. B   6. B   7. A   8. C   9. C   10. D

   11. B 12. C 13. A 14. B 15. D 16. C 17. B 18. D 19. C   20. C

6. 1. B   2. D   3. C   4. C   5. D

7. 1. Adapting to a new corporate culture is like fitting a pair of new shoes, which means there is no getting around it.

   2. The corporate culture refers to the operating work environment that is set and shaped by the executives and interwoven with processes, technologies, learning and significant events.

   3. The surface layer of corporate culture refers to visible cultures, which include the company dress code, work environment, work hours, ways for getting promoted, how the business world is viewed, what is valued and who is valued.

   4. Because invisible culture can influence an organization's competitiveness and management efficiencies.

   5. As a new member of the company, you can learn its corporate culture by observing how existing members behave and inferring what behaviors are appropriate and inappropriate.

8. 1. 在西方，明确和划分工作职责是营造浓厚的企业文化的手段。

   2. 国际贸易和海外投资的增加产生了对具有外语知识和跨文化交流技巧的管理人才的需求。

   3. 当在西方的商务场合中会见某人时，对话通常集中在一些商业事务或商业话题。

   4. 很明显，价值观的理念和差异影响了谈判的结果和谈判者的成功。

   5. 一个公司的文化决定和反映公司成员的价值观、信念和态度，这些价值观和信念构成员工的行为规范。

9. Koreans tend to base their business relationship on personal relations. The majority of Koreans stay with their first employer out of a sense of loyalty and mutual dependence. Loyalty in Korea is based on individual relations rather than group relations (for example, loyalty to a specific supervisor than to a company). The role of the inferior or employee is to obey the employer or superior's commands and to complete the task given by the superior without any objection. This has developed a strong paternalistic leadership in many Korean companies. As a result, a large proportion of Korean employee's life revolves around the workplace.

10.   The Most Important Thing in Cross-cultural Communication

   After China's entry into the WTO, Chinese people have more and more chances to direct communicate with people from other nations. In cross-cultural communication, many people believe that language is the biggest barrier, but I don't think so. In my opinion, the most important thing in cross-cultural communication is to show respect for others' culture.

My view on the importance of respecting your partner in cross-cultural communication lies in the fact that many failures are not caused by language misunderstanding but by cultural conflicts. For instance, it is impolite to ask English-speaking people questions about their age and salary, for these are their privacy. In China, however, these questions can show our concern for others. In speaking with people from a western culture, if we fail to show our respect for such a value of privacy, it may lead to communication failure.

Based on what is said above, it's not hard to understand the significance of the virtue of respect. If we are ignorant of cultural differences or show no respect for them, there will be no successful communication. Therefore, my suggestion for a foreign language learners is: learn a language as it is used in a culture.

Unit 9　*International Strategic Alliance*

1. 1. D　2. F　3. E　4. A　5. C　6. B

2. 1. B　2. D　3. C　4. A　5. C　6. A　7. D　8. D　9. A　10. C

3. 1. E　2. B　3. C　4. A　5. D

4. 1. C　2. E　3. A　4. D　5. B

5. 1. B　2. A　3. D　4. B　5. C　6. A　7. A　8. D　9. C　10. C
　 11. A　12. C　13. D　14. B　15. A　16. D　17. D　18. B　19. C　20. A

6. 1. B　2. B　3. C　4. C　5. C

7. 1. The main goal of the league is to "draw closer the relations between member states and coordinate collaboration between them, to safeguard their independence and sovereignty, and to consider in a general way the affairs and interests of the Arab countries."
　 2. The great fertile lands in southern Sudan.
　 3. The tourism industry.
　 4. The Gulf Cooperation Council (GCC).
　 5. Economic development in the Arab League is very disparate. Significant difference in wealth and economic conditions exist between the rich oil states of the UAE, Qatar, Kuwait, and Algeria on the one hand, and poor countries like the Comoros, Mauritania, and Djibouti on the other.

8. 1. 2010上半年世界商品贸易值相比2009年同期强势上升25％左右。
　 2. 维护地区的和平与稳定，发展经济和科技，扩大互利合作，促进共同繁荣，已成为东亚各国的共识。
　 3. 世贸组织总干事帕斯卡尔拉米在 2010年8月31日说 "现行多边贸易规则还是不均衡，依然有利于发达国家"。

4. 我们看到的每年APEC峰会所拍的合影里，一些世界各国有权势的政治家们所穿的服装风格各异，各具特色。

5. 非洲联盟的最高决策机构是首脑大会，由所有非洲联盟成员国政府首脑组成。

9. Some 99% of all European companies are small businesses, with fewer than 250 employees. As major employers and the main source of new jobs, they hold the key to getting the European economy back on a strong track. Small businesses and entrepreneurs need governments and Union to hold more of such activities to help and promote development of small business.

10.

China and APEC

Asia-Pacific Economic Cooperation (APEC) is a forum for 21 Pacific Rim countries to cooperate on regional trade and investment liberalization and facilitation. APEC's objective is to enhance economic growth and prosperity in the region and to strengthen the Asia-Pacific community. The member countries of APEC have been trying to achieve a level of economic development that may be sustained over the long run.

APEC is an important forum for China to show its commitment to economic openness. Concerted trade liberalization in the APEC region reduces the adverse terms of trade effect of China's own trade liberalization. It is shown that increased industrial growth in China — due to China integrating more into the global economy — would be beneficial to APEC, since it would boost industrialization in other Asian countries.

There are still strong reasons to believe that APEC will have a major impact on regional and global trade and it will be a vehicle for significant and highly beneficial trade liberalization. APEC remains an exciting opportunity — a process where some key decisions still need to be taken, but a process that can bring great benefit not just to all APEC members but to the rest of the world.

Unit 10 Cross-cultural Communication

1. 1. C   2. D   3. A   4. E   5. B

2. 1. D   2. A   3. A   4. D   5. C   6. B   7. C   8. A   9. D   10. D

3. 1. E   2. C   3. A   4. B   5. D   6. D   7. B   8. E   9. A   10. C

4. 1. D   2. E   3. B   4. A   5. C

5. 1. B   2. D   3. B   4. D   5. A   6. B   7. D   8. B   9. A   10. B
   11. C 12. B 13. C 14. B 15. A 16. A 17. D 18. C 19. B   20. D

6. 1. A   2. C   3. B   4. B   5. D

7. 1. A sense of humor.
   2. Because they show that certain comic stereotypes have a universal appeal.
   3. One of the chief functions of irony and satire is to redress balance.

4. Because human beings all share the ability to laugh although they oppose each other on a great many issues.

5. A happy, courageous and initiative life.

8. 1. 提高学习能力和学习质量是解决人力资源、跨文化管理等问题的有效方法之一。

   2. 全新的企业文化是解决跨文化团队管理问题的最终答案。

   3. 本书作者阐明了文化，特别是作为文化一部分的普世文化在帮助学生理解词的内涵意义和获取文化的基本途径方面所起的重要作用，这有助于培养学生跨文化交际意识。

   4. 我们探讨了文化因素对人格的深远影响，并将跨文化研究和有关文化与民族差异的讨论结合起来。

   5. 一般而言，公司文化是指导我们进行日常商业决策的指南针。

9. Because Mr. Tanaka doesn't realize cultural differences in a foreign country.

   This case tells us that people from different culture backgrounds should keep a strong sense of cross-cultural awareness. The problems mentioned in this case are very common with people doing international business. No matter what staffing patterns a company adopts, they may probably confront such communication problems. Therefore, to ensure successful trade with business partners, both sides should have a comprehensive understanding of the host culture and the guest culture, especially the differences between them, and adapt themselves to the new culture environments, definitely avoiding solving problems partially based on their native culture.

   In this case, for lack of cross-cultural awareness, the Japanese felt that he was misunderstood and coldly treated.

10.

April 2, 2010

Mr. White,

As a long-time member of the Downtown Marketing Club, I have enjoyed and benefited from the luncheon speakers the Club sponsors each month. Many talks are fairly interesting and meaningful.

As you may have read in the newspaper, our company is opening an outlet in China, and I will be there May 1 – 10 interviewing marketing representatives and setting up sales territories. Thus, you will need to select another speaker for the next time performance.

If you find yourself in need of a speaker during the summer months, Mr. White, please keep me in mind. My business schedule thus far is quite light during June, July and August.

Sincerely,

×××

郑重声明

高等教育出版社依法对本书享有专有出版权。任何未经许可的复制、销售行为均违反《中华人民共和国著作权法》，其行为人将承担相应的民事责任和行政责任；构成犯罪的，将被依法追究刑事责任。为了维护市场秩序，保护读者的合法权益，避免读者误用盗版书造成不良后果，我社将配合行政执法部门和司法机关对违法犯罪的单位和个人进行严厉打击。社会各界人士如发现上述侵权行为，希望及时举报，本社将奖励举报有功人员。

反盗版举报电话　　（010）58581897 58582371 58581879
反盗版举报传真　　（010）82086060
反盗版举报邮箱　　dd@hep.com.cn
通信地址　　北京市西城区德外大街4号　高等教育出版社法务部
邮政编码　　100120

短信防伪说明

本图书采用出版物短信防伪系统，用户购书后刮开封底防伪密码涂层，将16位防伪密码发送短信至106695881280，免费查询所购图书真伪，同时您将有机会参加鼓励使用正版图书的抽奖活动，赢取各类奖项，详情请查询中国扫黄打非网（http://www.shdf.gov.cn）。

反盗版短信举报

编辑短信"JB，图书名称，出版社，购买地点"发送至10669588128

短信防伪客服电话

（010）58582300